EASY PIANO

MOVIE SHEET MUSIC HITS

Arranged by DAN COATES

T5-ADA-297

Product Line Manager: Carol Cuellar
Project Manager: Donna Salzburg
Cover Design: Joe Klucar

Dan Coates® is a registered trademark of Warner Bros. Publications

© 2004 WARNER BROS. PUBLICATIONS
All Rights Reserved

Any duplication, adaptation or arrangement of the compositions
contained in this collection requires the written consent of the Publisher.
No part of this book may be photocopied or reproduced in any way without permission.
Unauthorized uses are an infringement of the U.S. Copyright Act and are punishable by law.

CONTENTS

Across the Stars
Star Wars®: Episode II *Attack of the Clones* 8

And All That Jazz
Chicago 3

Arthur's Theme (The Best That You Can Do)
Arthur 12

Because You Loved Me
Up Close & Personal 16

Come What May
Moulin Rouge 21

The Entertainer
The Sting 30

Eye of the Tiger
Rocky III 26

Fawkes the Phoenix
Harry Potter and the Chamber of Secrets 33

Gollum's Song
The Lord of the Rings: The Two Towers 36

Hedwig's Theme
Harry Potter and the Sorcerer's Stone 40

How Do I Live
Con Air 44

I Believe I Can Fly
Space Jam 48

I Don't Want to Miss a Thing
Armageddon 52

In Dreams
The Lord of the Rings: The Fellowship of the Ring 56

James Bond Theme
Die Another Day 62

Over the Rainbow
The Wizard of Oz 66

Somewhere, My Love (Lara's Theme)
Dr. Zhivago 59

Somewhere Out There
An American Tail 69

Star Wars (Main Title)
Star Wars® 72

Stayin' Alive
Saturday Night Fever 74

Tears in Heaven
Rush 78

That's What Friends Are For
Night Shift 82

Theme From Ice Castles (Through the Eyes of Love)
Ice Castles 87

There You'll Be
Pearl Harbor 90

The Wind Beneath My Wings
Beaches 95

AND ALL THAT JAZZ

Words by
FRED EBB

Music by
JOHN KANDER
Arranged by DAN COATES

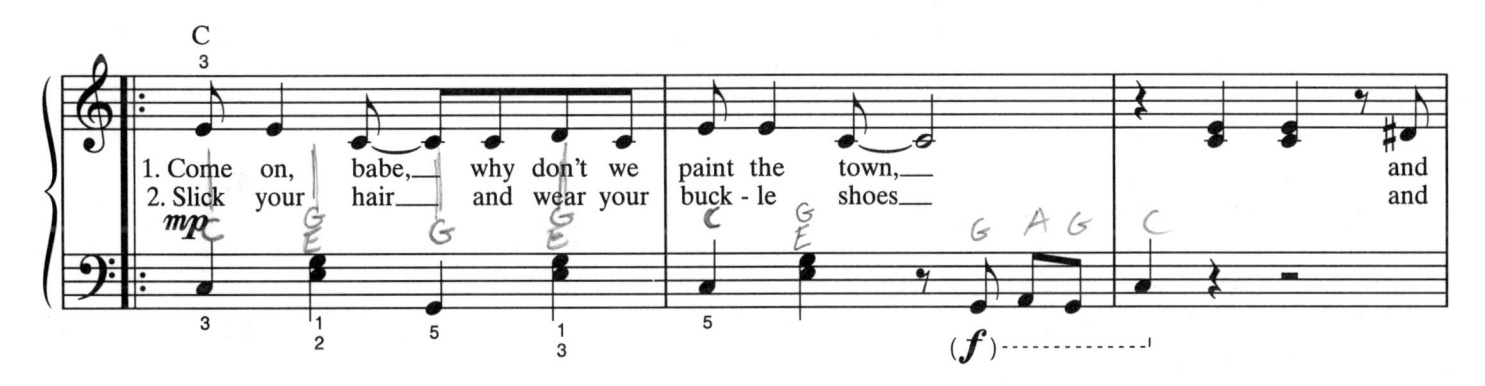

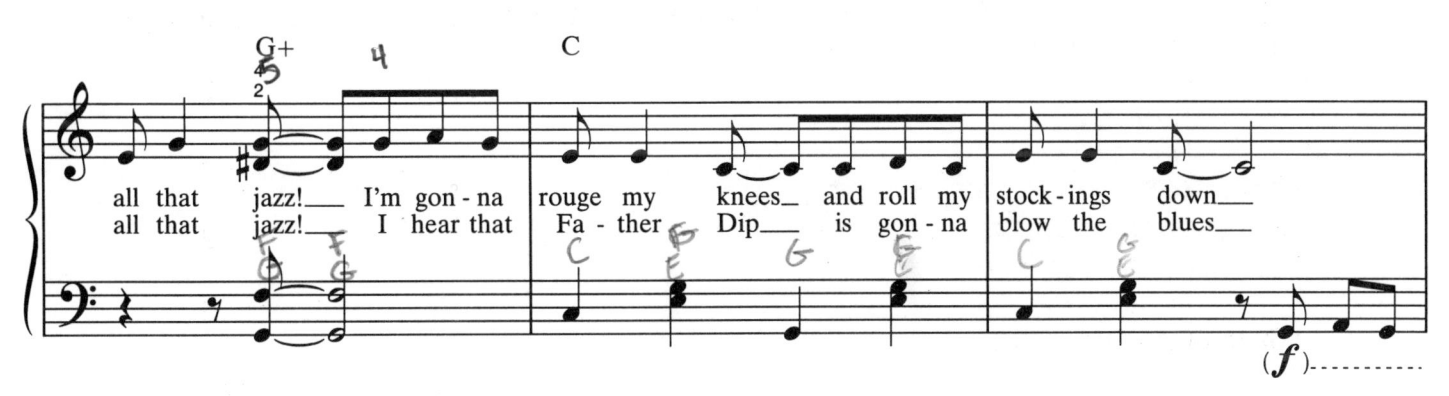

Moderately, with a deliberate beat

1. Come on, babe, why don't we paint the town, and all that jazz! I'm gonna rouge my knees and roll my stockings down and all that jazz! Start the car, I know a

2. Slick your hair and wear your buckle shoes and all that jazz! I hear that Father Dip is gonna blow the blues and all that jazz! Hold on, hon, we're gonna

And All That Jazz - 5 - 1

© 1975 KANDER & EBB, INC. and UNICHAPPELL MUSIC INC.
Copyright Renewed
All Rights Administered by UNICHAPPELL MUSIC INC.
All Rights Reserved including Public Performance

4

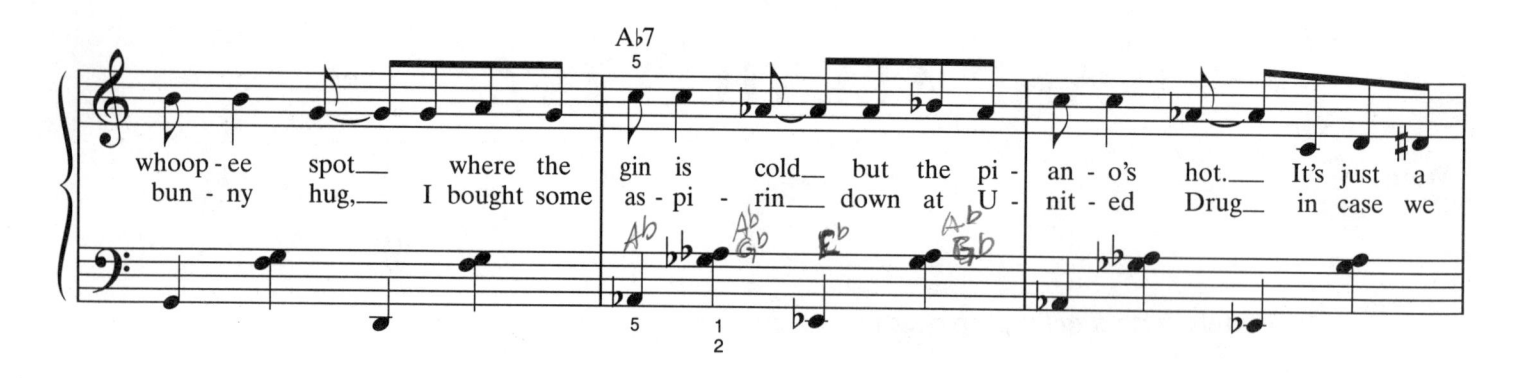

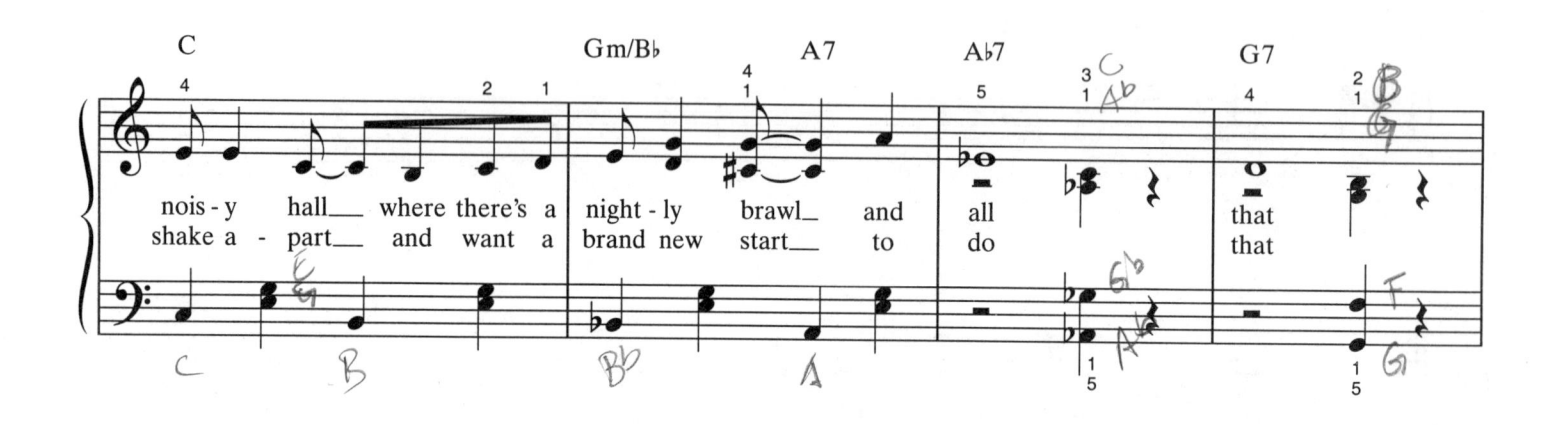

all that jazz!)
Oh,
she' gon-na shim-my 'til her
gar-ters break. (And
all that jazz!)
A7
Show
her where to park her gir-dle,
B♭7
oh,
her moth-er's blood-'d cur-dle
D
D/C♯
D/C
B7
E7(♭9)
A7
if she'd hear her
ba-by's queer for
all
that
dim.
mp

D
jazz!
G7
C
Find a flask,_ we're play-ing
fast and loose_ and all that jazz!_
Right up here_ is where I store the juice,_ and all that jazz!_
G7
Come on, babe,_ we're gon - na brush the sky._ I bet-cha
A♭7
luck - y Lin - dy nev - er flew so high,_ 'cause in the
C
C/B
stra-to - sphere_ how could he

C/B♭ A7 A♭7 G7 C
lend an ear__ to all that jazz!
mf
cresc.
G Am7 G/B C C/B
No, I'm no one's wife,__ but
f
C/B♭ A7 D7
oh, I love my life__ and all
ff
G7
that
C C/B♭ F/A Fm/A♭ C/G G7 C
jazz!
fff
That jazz!
sfz

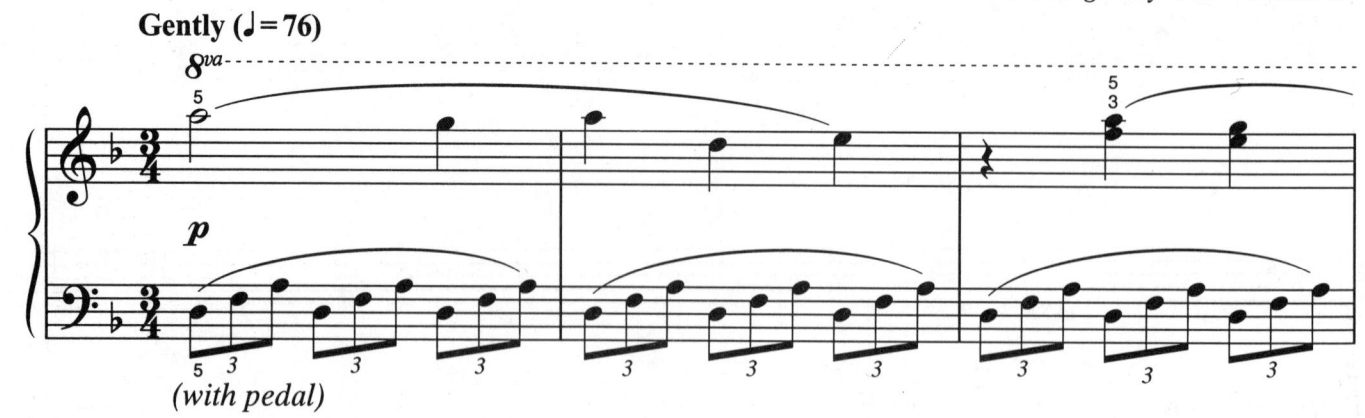

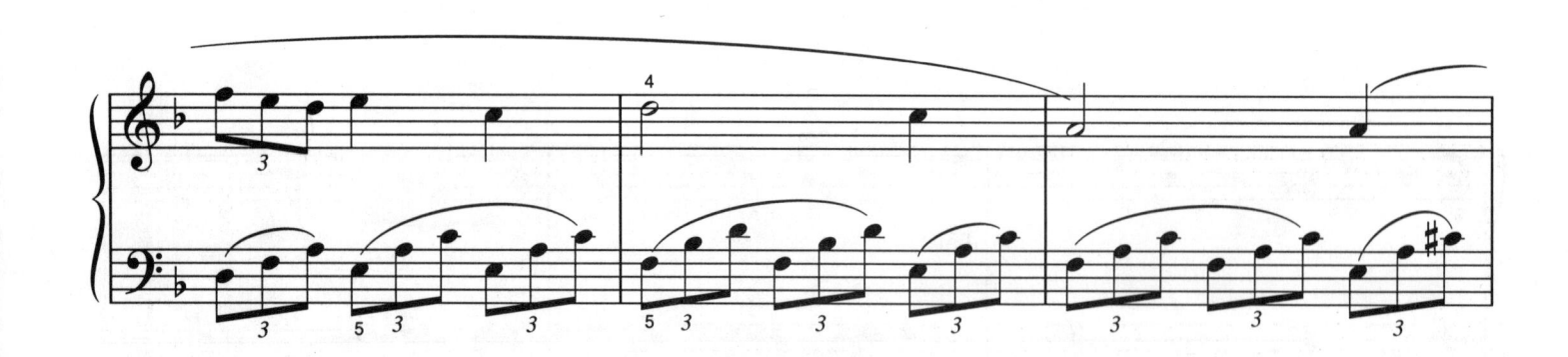

ACROSS THE STARS
(LOVE THEME FROM *STAR WARS* ®: EPISODE II)

Music by
JOHN WILLIAMS
Arranged by DAN COATES

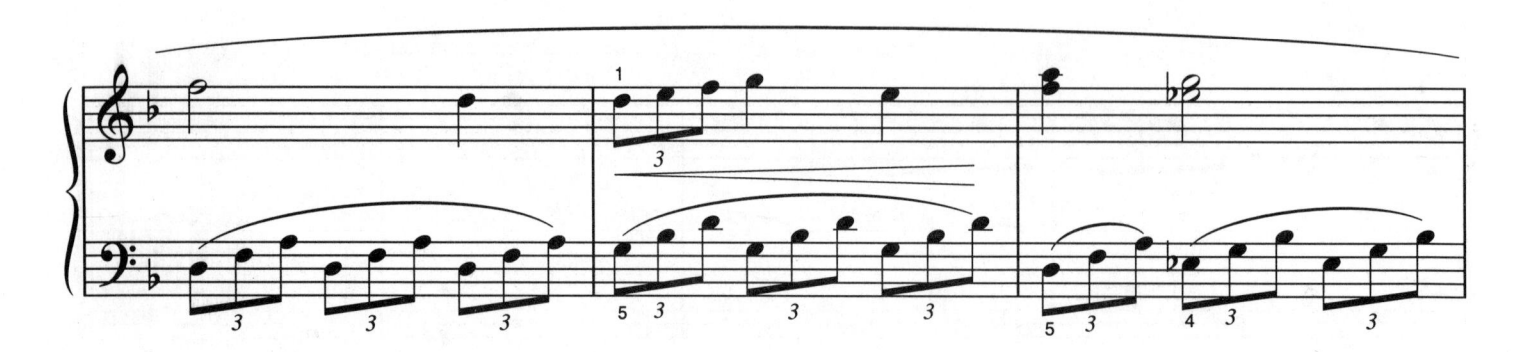

9

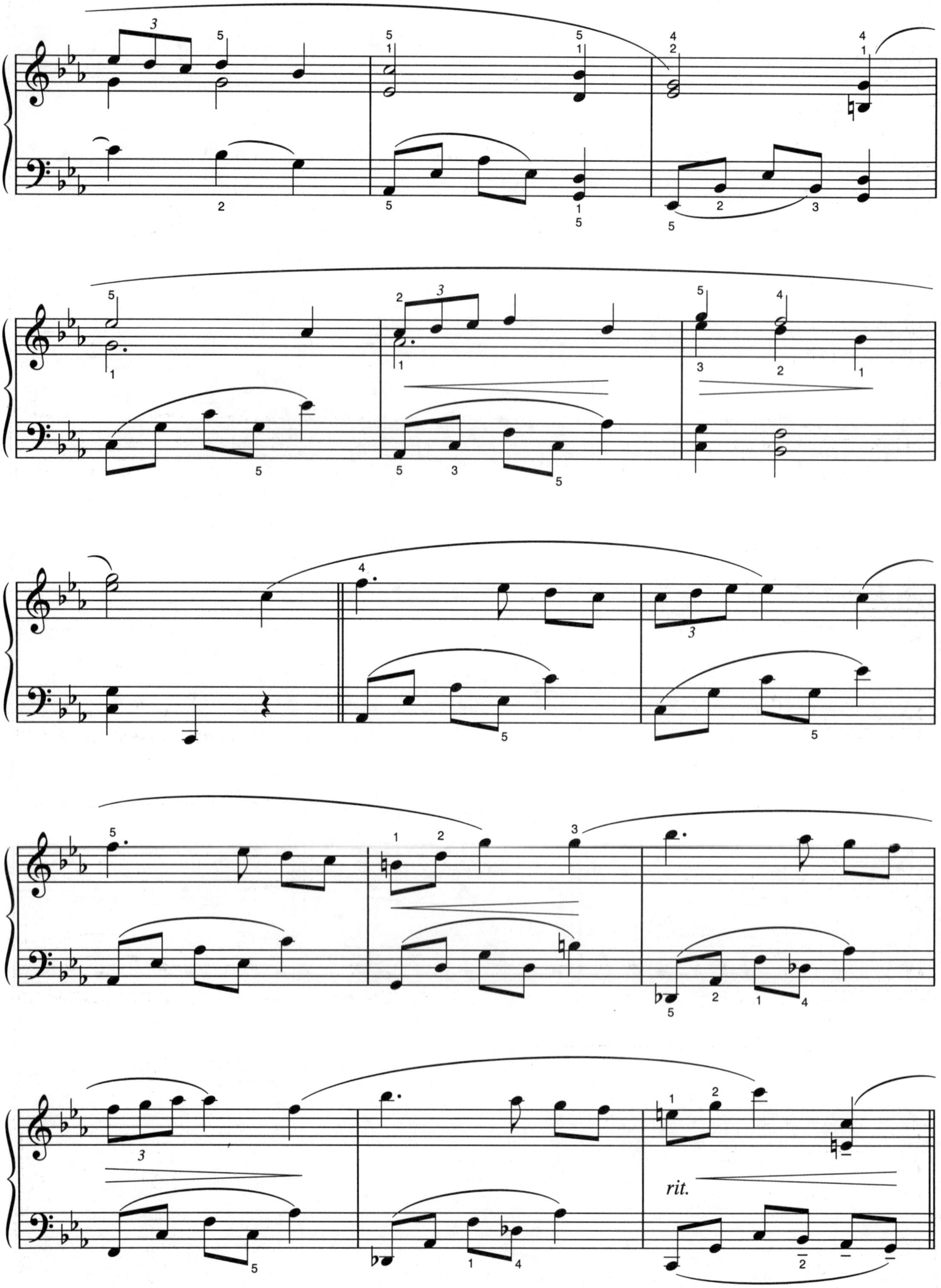
rit.

Appassionato

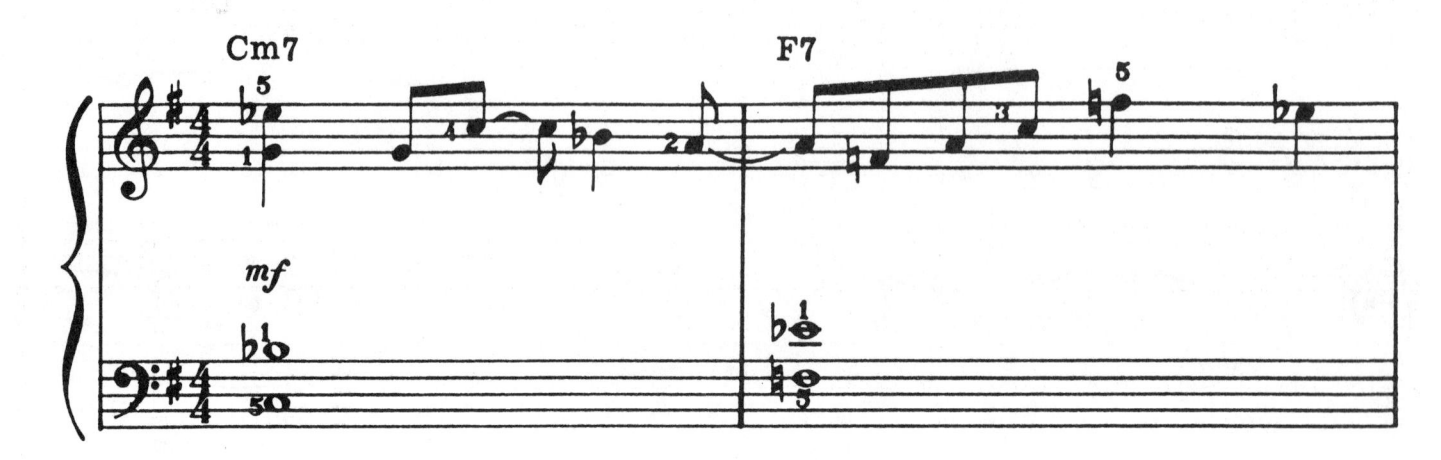

ARTHUR'S THEME

(Best That You Can Do)

Words and Music by
PETER ALLEN, CAROLE BAYER SAGER,
CHRISTOPHER CROSS and BURT BACHARACH
Arranged by DAN COATES

Moderately

Cm7
F7
Bb
Once in your life, you'll find her, some-one who turns your
Ar-thur, he does what he pleas-es. All of his life, his
mf
Eb
Ab
D7
heart a - round, and next thing you know, you're clos - in'
mas - ter's toys, and deep in his heart, he's just, he's
G
D/G G G/B Cm7
down the town.
just a boy.
Wake up and she's still with
Liv - in' his life one day
F7
Bb
Eb
you, e - ven though you left her way a - cross town. You're
at a time, he's show-in' him - self a real-ly good time. He's

won-der - in' to___ your - self, hey, what-'ve I found?
laugh- in' a - bout_ the way they want him to be._

When you get caught be- tween the moon and New York City,___ I know it's cra - zy, but it's true._

Cmaj7 D/C C Bm7
If you get caught_ be -tween the moon and New York Cit - y,
E7sus E7 Am7
the best that you can do,___ the
best that you_ can do___ is fall_ in
1. C
love.___
G G/B
mf
2. C G/B Am7 G
love.
rit.
mp

BECAUSE YOU LOVED ME

Words and Music by
DIANE WARREN
Arranged by DAN COATES

Slowly ♩ = 66

1. For all those times you stood by me, for all the truth that you made me see, for all the joy you brought to my life, for all the wrong that you made right. For ev'ry dream you made come true, for all the love I found in you, I'll

wings and made me fly, you touched my hand, I could touch the sky. I lost my faith, you gave it back to me. You said no star was out of reach. You stood by me and I stood tall. I had your love, I had it all. I'm

Because You Loved Me - 5 - 1

© 1996 REALSONGS (ASCAP) and TOUCHSTONE PICTURES SONGS & MUSIC, INC. (ASCAP)
All Rights Reserved

Gm7/C
E♭
Dm7
be for - ev - er thank - ful, ba - by. You're the one who held
grate - ful for each day you gave me. May - be I don't know
mf
Gm7
me up, nev - er let me fall.
that much, but I know this much is true:
B♭m7
B♭/C
You're the one who saw me through, through it all.
I was blessed be - cause I was loved by you.
F
You were my strength when I was weak, you were my
mp

voice when I could-n't speak. You were my eyes when I could-n't see, you saw the best there was in me. Lift-ed me up when I could-n't reach, you gave me faith 'cause you be-lieved. I'm ev-'ry-thing I am be-cause you

1.
F
B♭/C
loved me.
2. You gave me
mp
2.
F
A7
loved me.
You were al - ways there
mp
mf
Dm7
for me, the ten - der wind that car - ried me. A
A7
Dm
light in the dark,
shin - ing your love in - to my life.

Gm7
You've been my in - spi - ra - tion, through the
f
F/A
C7sus4
lies, you were the truth. My world is a bet - ter place
B♭/C
D.S. al Coda
because of you. You were my
Coda
F
Gm7/C
loved me. I'm ev - 'ry - thing I am
mp
F
be - cause you loved me.
p

COME WHAT MAY

Words and Music by
DAVID BAERWALD
Arranged by DAN COATES

Am D7 Dm7/G
Lis - ten to my heart. Can you hear it sing, tell - ing me to give you
F/C C Am Am/G D/F♯
ev - 'ry - thing. Sea - sons may change, win - ter to spring,
D C Dm7/G G
but I'll love you un - til the end of
C
time. Come what
cresc.
Chorus:
Am
may, come what
mf

23

Verse 2:

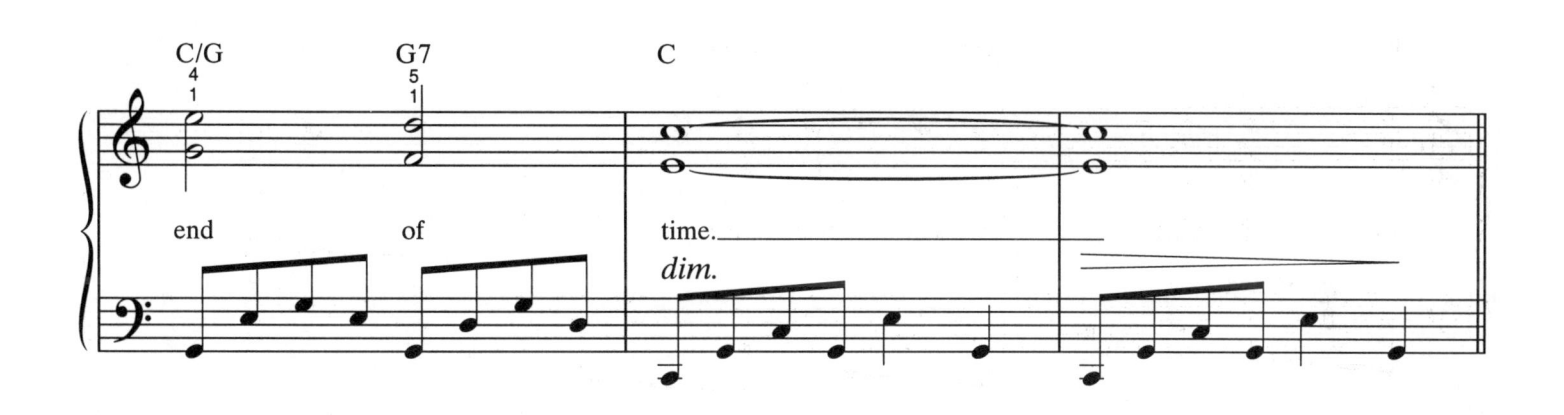

2. Sud-den-ly the world seems such a per-fect place. Sud-den-ly it moves with such a per-fect grace. Sud-den-ly my life does-n't seem such a waste.

may, I will love you un-til the end of time.

dim.

mp

Come What May - 5 - 3

F C Am
It all re-volves a - round you. And there's no moun-tain too high, no
D Dm7/G F/C C
riv - er too wide. Sing out this song and I'll be there by your side.
Am Am/G D/F♯ D
Storm clouds may gath - er, and stars may col - lide. But I'll
C Dm7/G G C
love you un - til the end of time. Come what
cresc.

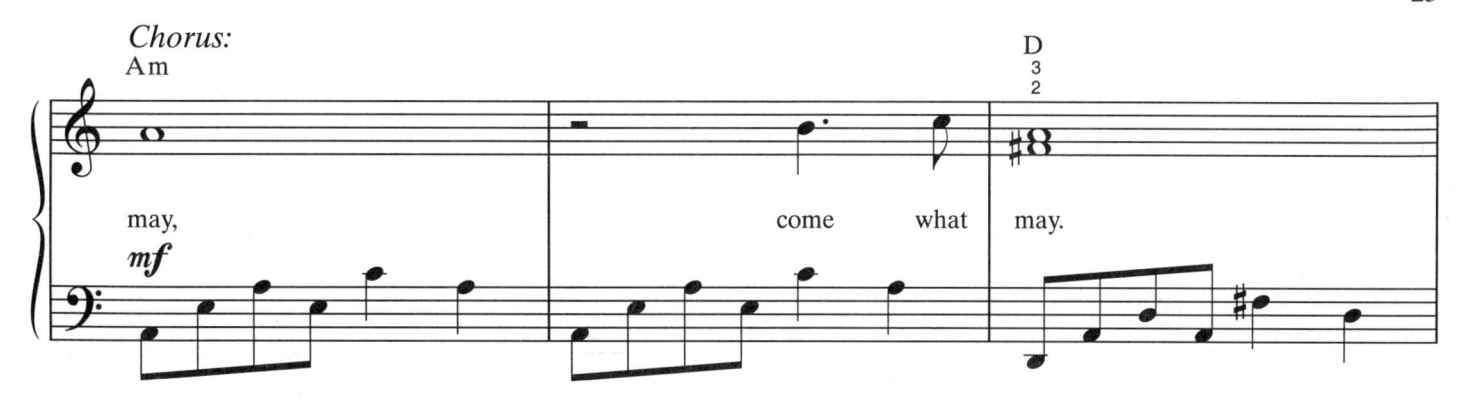

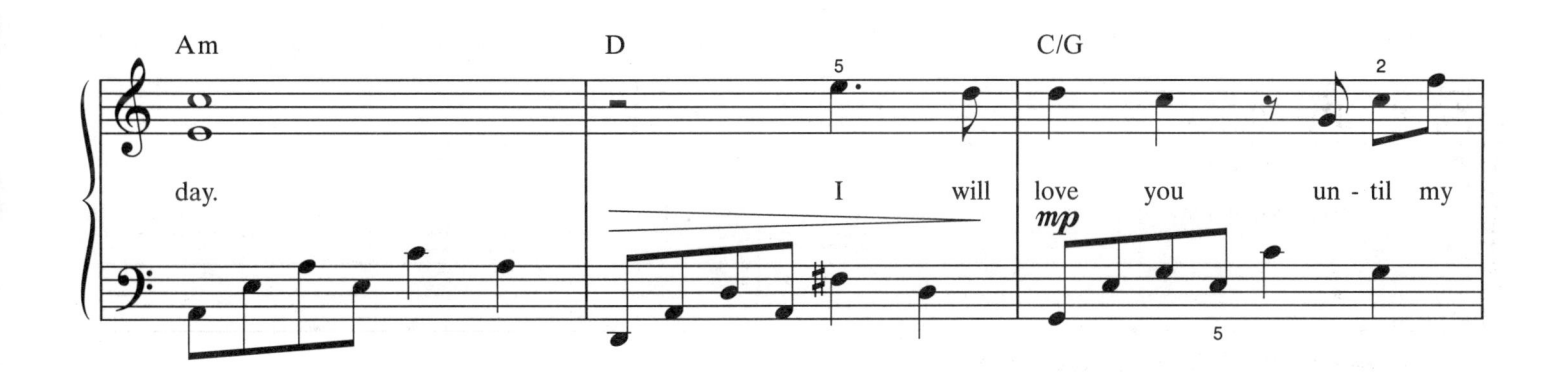

Come What May - 5 - 5

EYE OF THE TIGER
The Theme from ROCKY III

Words and Music by
FRANKIE SULLIVAN III and JIM PETERIK
Arranged by DAN COATES

Went the dis-tance. Now I'm back on my feet, just a man and his will to sur-vive.

1. So man-y times it hap-pens too fast.
2. Face to face, out in the heat,

You trade your pas-sion for glo-ry.
hang-in' tough, stay-in' hun-gry.

Ab/C
Don't lose your grip on the dreams of the past. You must
They stack the odds, still we take to the street for the
Bb/C
Cm
Bb
Cm
fight just to keep them a - live.
kill with the will to sur - vive.
It's the
Chorus:
Fm
Eb/G
Bb
Cm
eye of the ti - ger. It's the thrill of the fight, ris - in'
f
Fm
Cm
Bb
Cm
up to the chal-lenge of our ri - val. And the
Fm
Eb/G
Bb
Cm
last known sur - vi - vor stalks his prey in the night, and he's

Additional Lyrics

3. Risin' up, straight to the top.
   Had the guts, got the glory.
   Went the distance. Now I'm not gonna stop,
   just a man and his will to survive.

(To Chorus)

THE ENTERTAINER

By
SCOTT JOPLIN
Arranged by DAN COATES

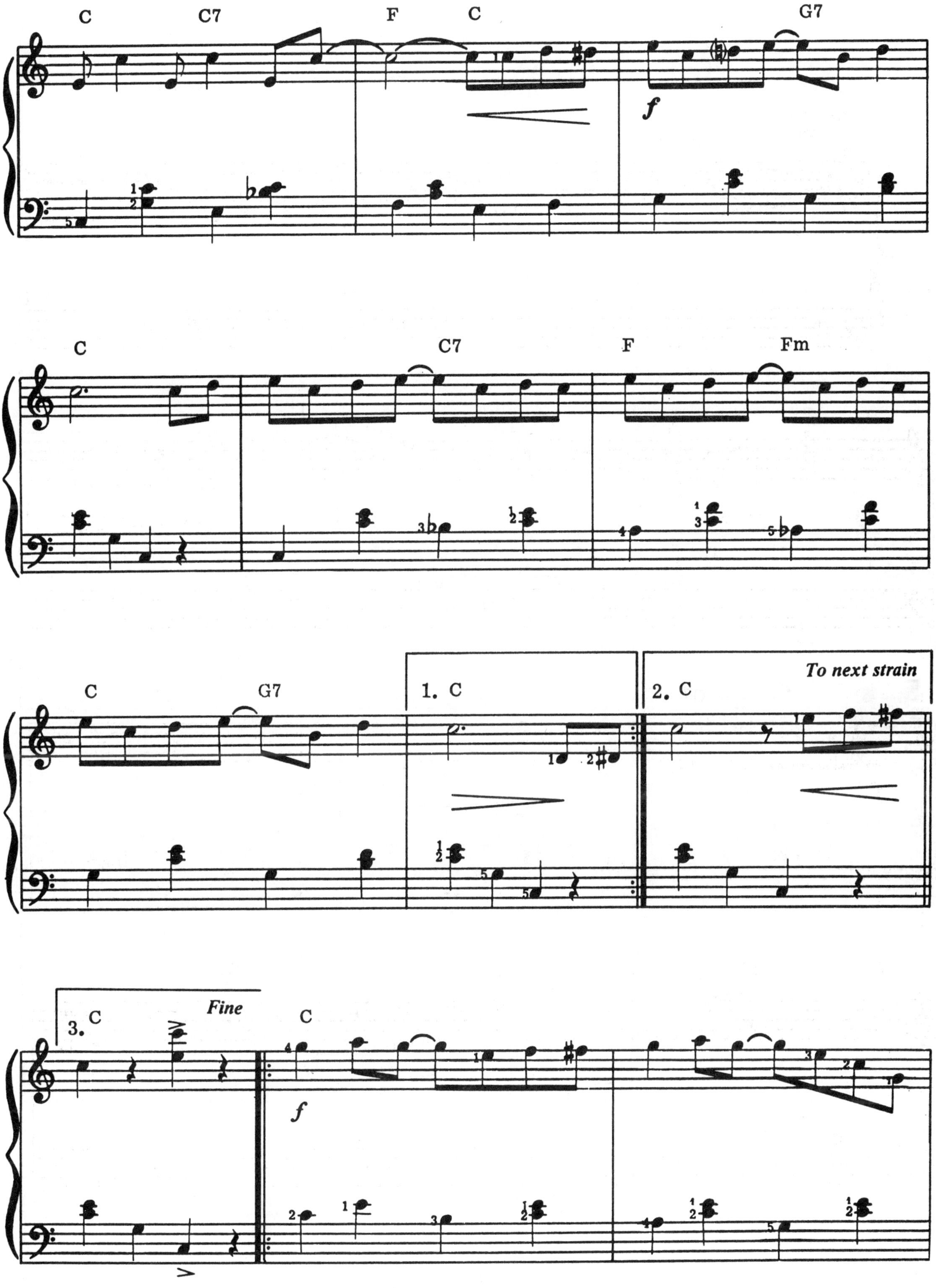
C
C7
F
C
G7
f
C
C7
F
Fm
C
G7
1. C
2. C
To next strain
3. C
Fine
C
f

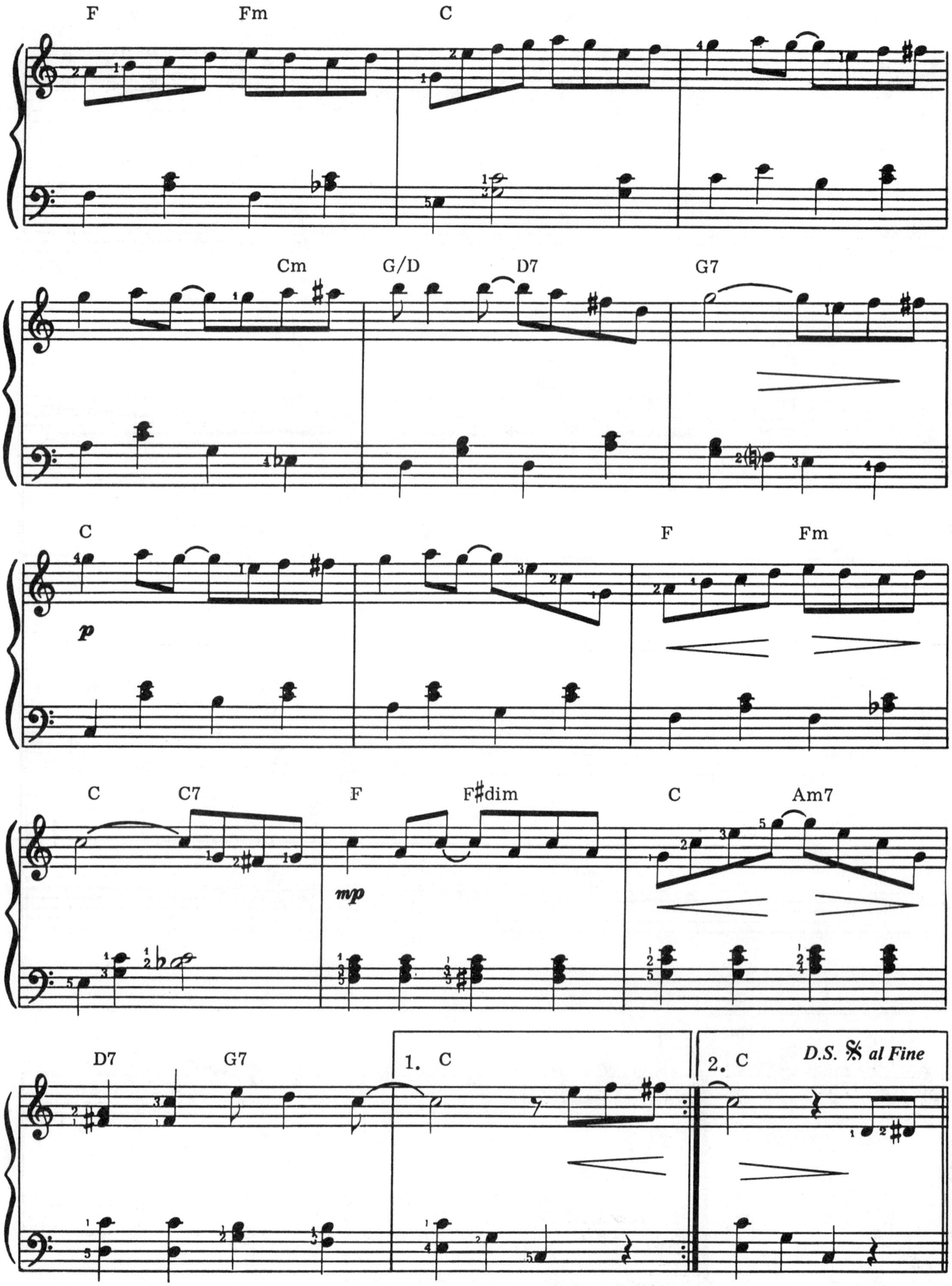
F
Fm
C
Cm
G/D
D7
G7
C
p
F
Fm
C
C7
F
F♯dim
mp
C
Am7
D7
G7
1. C
2. C
D.S. 𝄋 al Fine

FAWKES THE PHOENIX

Music by
JOHN WILLIAMS
Arranged by DAN COATES

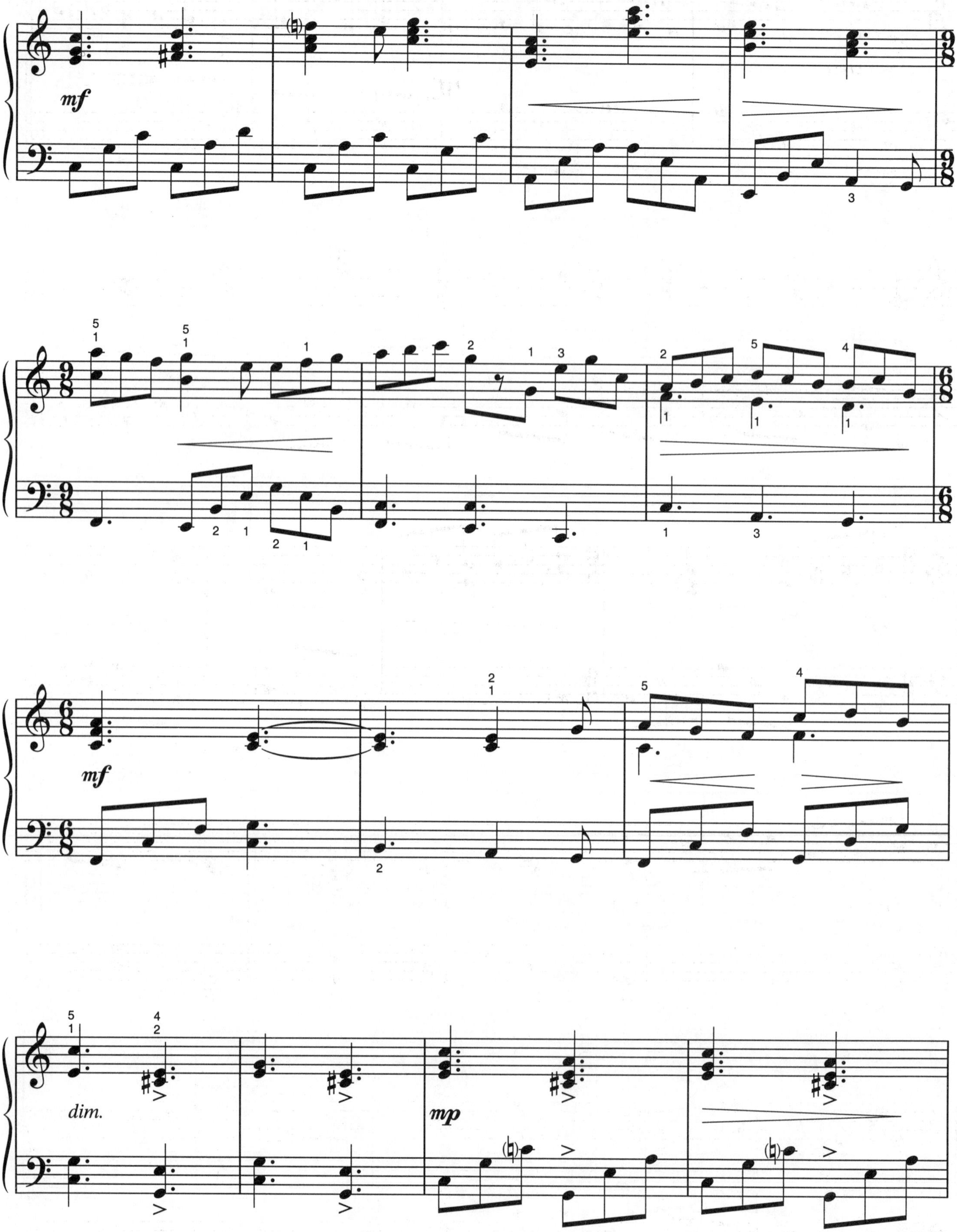
mf
mf
dim.
mp

Fawkes the Phoenix

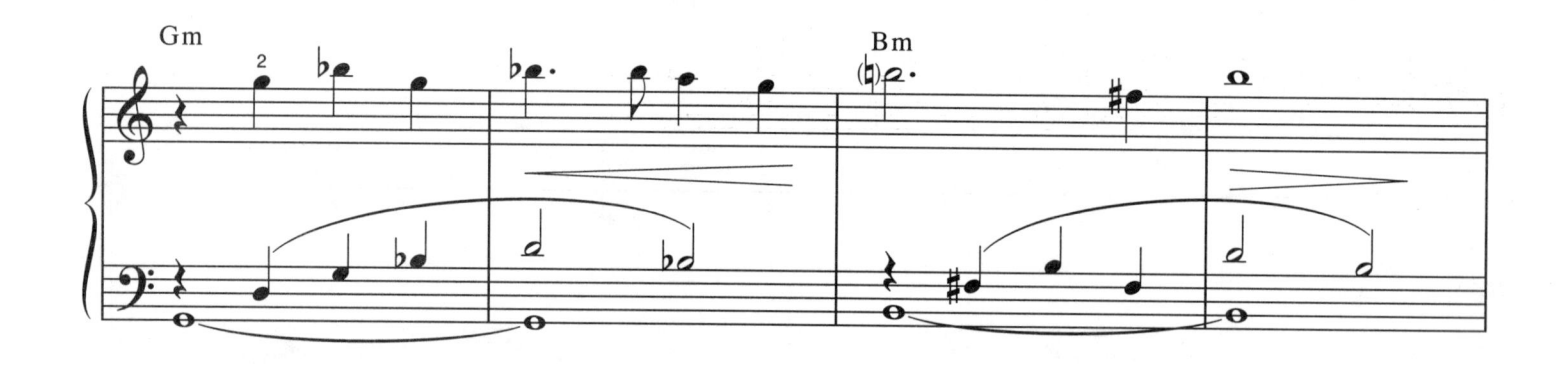

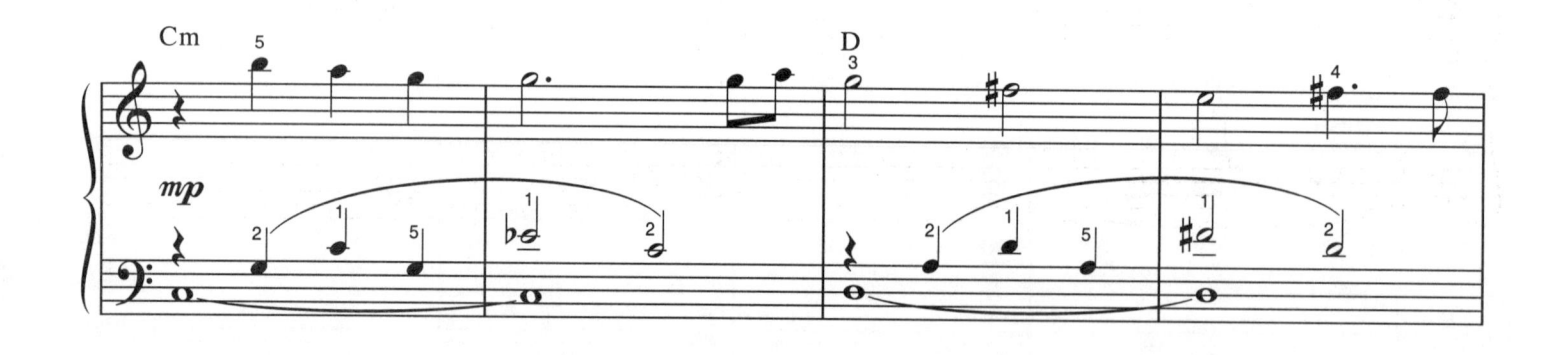

GOLLUM'S SONG
as performed by Emiliana Torrini in the motion picture
"The Lord of the Rings: The Two Towers"

Words by FRAN WALSH
Music by HOWARD SHORE
Arranged by DAN COATES

Moderately slow (♩ = 104)

p legato

(with pedal)

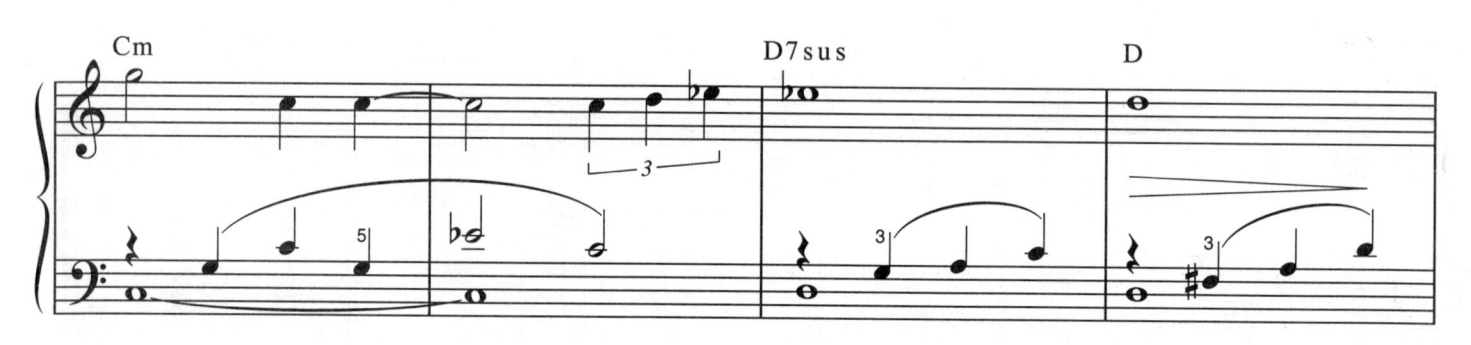

37

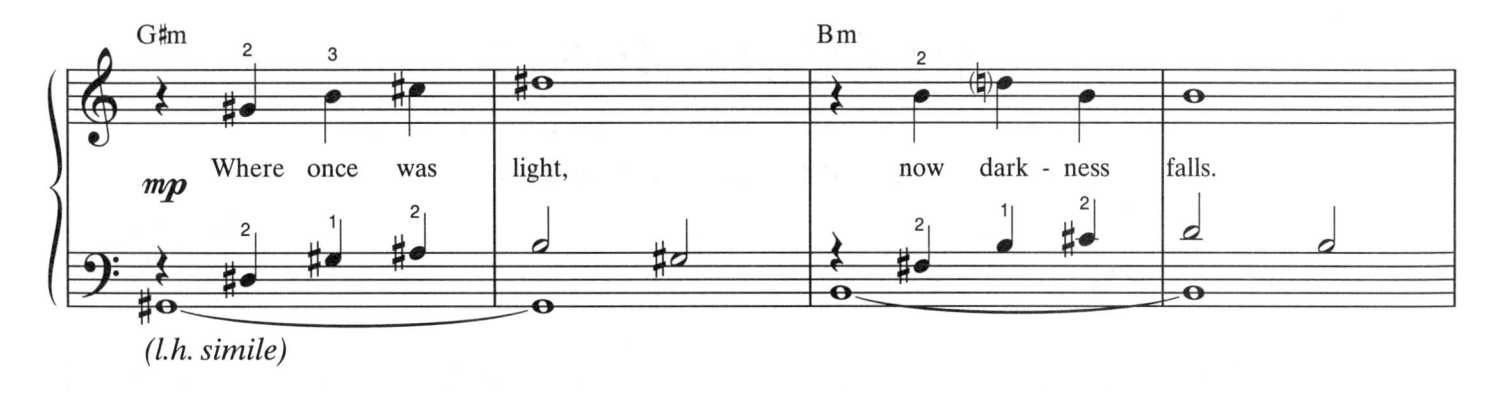

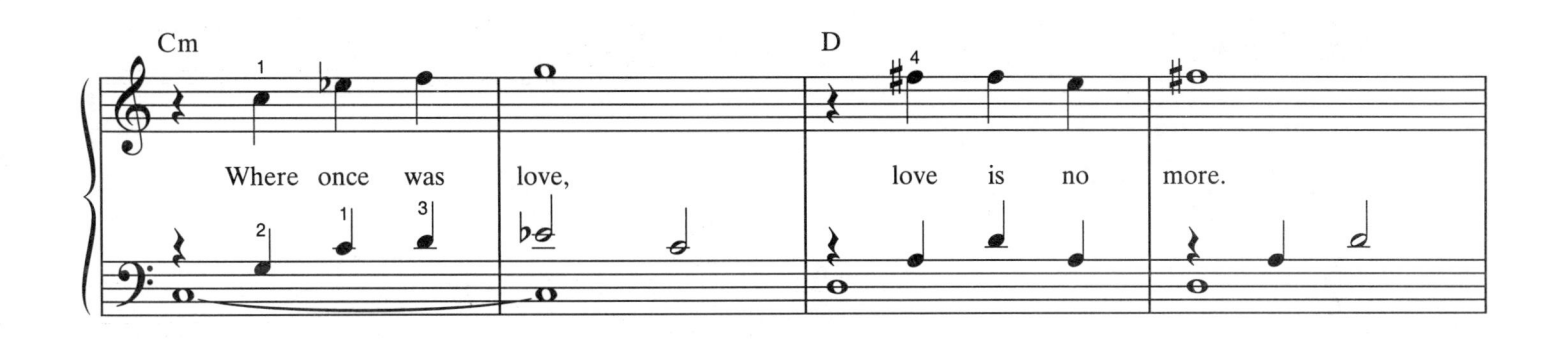

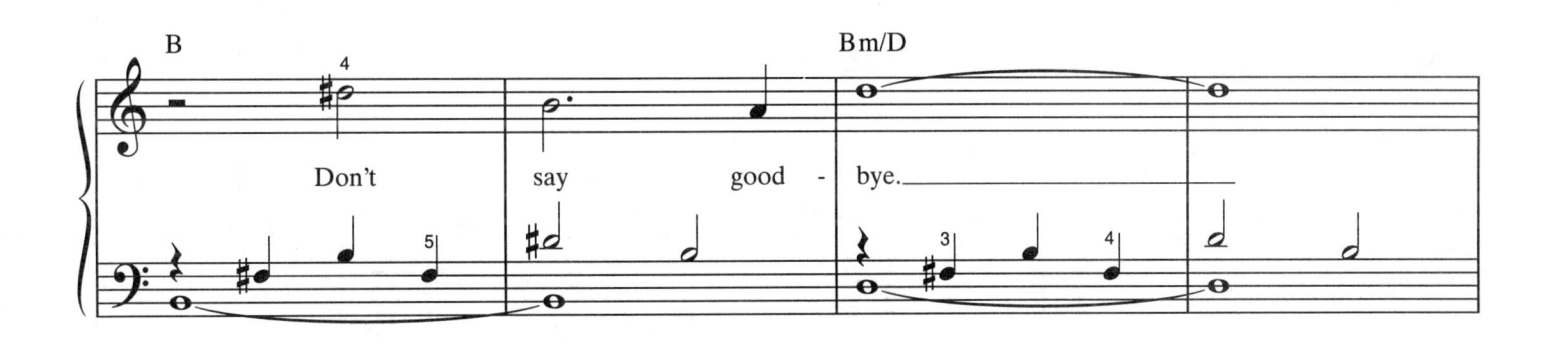

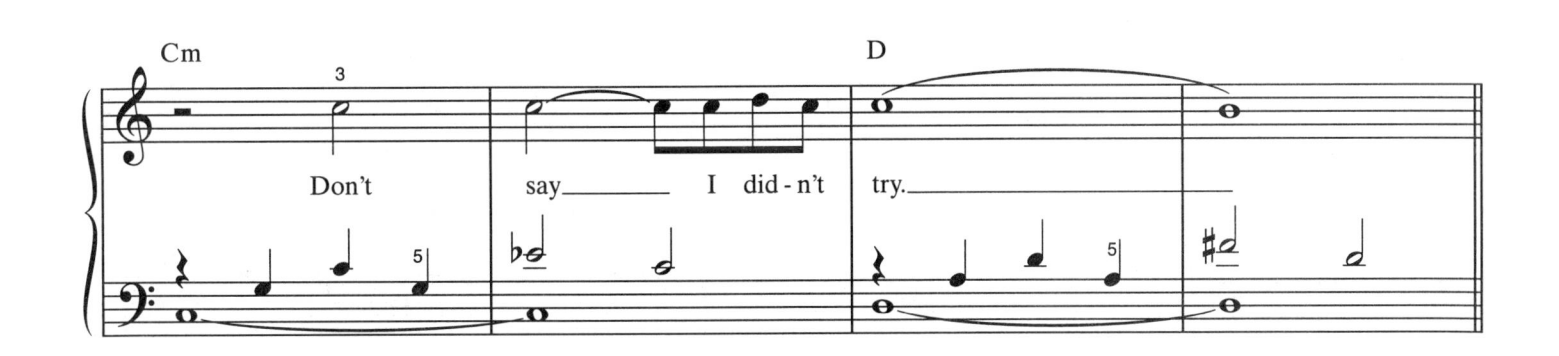

Gm
Bm
These tears we cry are fall - ing rain,
These tears you cry have come too late.
mf
Gm
Bm
for all the lies you told us, the hurt, the blame.
Take back the lies, the hurt, the blame.
Cm
D
To Coda
And we will weep to be so a - lone. We are
And you will weep when you face the end a - lone. You are
Cm
D
lost. We can nev - er go home.
G♯m
Bm
So in the end I'll be what I will be.
mp

Cm
D
No loy - al friend was ev - er there for me.
B
Bm/D
mf
Now we say good - bye.
Cm
D7sus
D
D.S. 𝄋 al Coda
We say you did - n't try.
𝄌 Coda
Cm
D
lost. You can nev - er go home. You are
dim.
Cm
D
lost. You can nev - er go home.
mp
rit.
p

From Warner Bros. Pictures' HARRY POTTER AND THE SORCERER'S STONE

HEDWIG'S THEME

Music by
JOHN WILLIAMS
Arranged by DAN COATES

Misterioso (♩. = 58)

41

Hedwig's Theme - 4 - 2

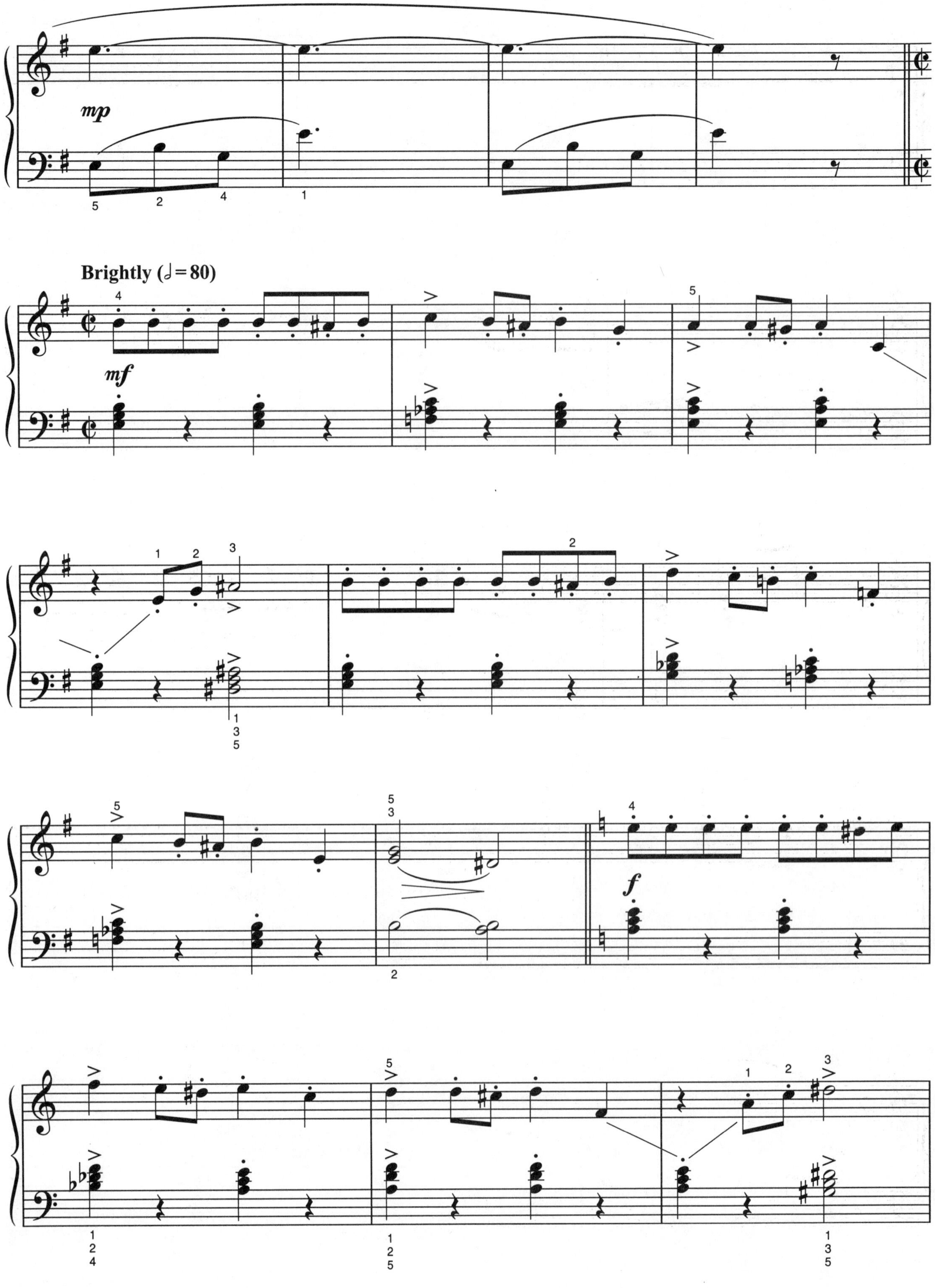
mp
Brightly (𝅗𝅥 = 80)
mf
f

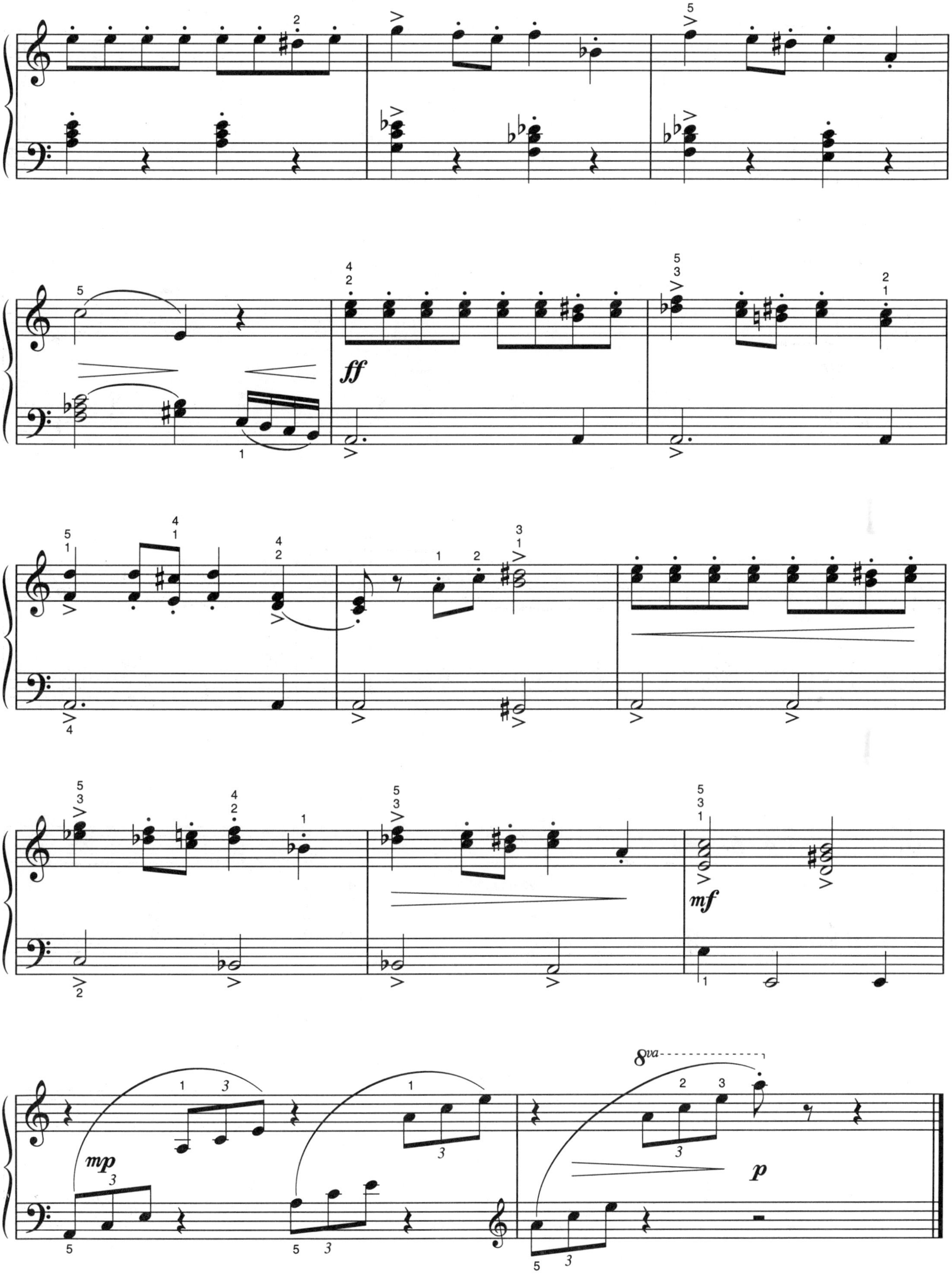
ff
mf
mp
8va
p

HOW DO I LIVE

Words and Music by
DIANE WARREN
Arranged by DAN COATES

C Bm7 Em7
world, my heart, my soul. If you ev - er leave,
cresc.
Am7 Bm7 Em7 B♭/C C7
ba - by, you would take a - way ev - 'ry - thing good in my life. And tell me
F C B♭ C7 F C
now, how do I live with - out you? I want to know. How do I breathe with - out
mf
B♭ Am7 Dm Gm7 Am7 B♭
you, if you ev - er go? How do I ev - er, ev - er sur - vive?

To Coda
1.
Gm7/C
F
C/D
How do I,
how do I,
oh, how do I
live?
2. With - out you
mp
2.
Gm7/C
F
Am7
Gm7
how do I,
oh, how do I
live?
mp
Dm7
Am7
D7sus4
D7
cresc.
If
Bm7
Em7
Am7
you ev - er leave,
ba - by, you would take a - way ev - 'ry - thing.
mf

Verse 2:
Without you, there'd be no sun in my sky,
There would be no love in my life,
There'd be no world left for me.
And I, baby, I don't know what I would do,
I'd be lost if I lost you.
If you ever leave,
Baby, you would take away everything
Real in my life.
And tell me now...
(To Chorus:)

I BELIEVE I CAN FLY

Words and Music by
R. KELLY
Arranged by DAN COATES

Lyrics:
I used to think that I could not go on, and life was nothing but an awful song. But now I know the meaning of true love. I'm leaning on the everlasting arm. If I can

I was on the verge of breaking down. Sometimes silence can seem so loud. There are miracles in life I must achieve, but first I know it starts inside of me.

© 1996 ZOMBA SONGS INC./R. KELLY PUBLISHING, INC. (Adm. by ZOMBA SONGS INC.) (BMI)
All Rights Reserved

49

Am7
Dm7(♭5)
soar, I see me run - ning through that o - pen door. I be - lieve I can
C/G
Fm/G
To Coda
fly, I be - lieve I can fly, I be - lieve I can
dim.
mf
1.
Am
F/G
2.
Am
fly. See, fly.
mp
mp
Dm7
C/E
F
E7
Hey, 'cause I be - lieve in me. If I can

Am7
see it, then I can
mf
Fm/A♭
do it, if I just be-
C/G
lieve it, there's noth - ing
D.S. al Coda
G7
to it. I be - lieve I can
Coda
C/G
fly. If I just
mp
Fm/A♭
spread my wings, I can
C/G
fly. If I just
Fm/G
spread my wings, I can
C
fly.
Fm/A♭
rit. e dim.
C
p

From Touchstone Pictures' "ARMAGEDDON"

I DON'T WANT TO MISS A THING

**Words and Music by
DIANE WARREN**
Arranged by DAN COATES

Slowly ♩ = 68

1. I could stay a-wake just to hear you breath-ing, watch you smile while you are sleep-ing, while you're far a-way and dream-ing. I could spend my life in this sweet sur-ren-der. I could

close to you, feel-ing your heart beat-ing, and I'm won-d'ring what you're dream-ing, won-d'ring if it's me you're see-ing. Then I kiss your eyes and thank God we're to-geth-er. I just wan-na

I Don't Want to Miss a Thing - 4 - 1

© 1998 REALSONGS (ASCAP)
All Rights Reserved

1st time only
G D/F♯ Em
stay lost in this mo - ment for - ev - er. Ev - 'ry mo - ment
F♯m Gmaj7 A7sus4
spent with you is a mo - ment I treas - ure.
stay with you in this mo - ment for - ev - er.
D A/C♯ Em
mf
Don't wan - na close my eyes, don't wan - na fall a - sleep, 'cause I'd
G A7 D A/C♯
miss you, babe, and I don't wan - na miss a thing. 'Cause e - ven when I dream of you,

To Coda
Em
the sweet - est dream would nev - er do. I'd still
1.
G
A7
miss you, babe, and I don't wan - na miss a thing.
D
A
G
mp
2. Lay - ing
2.
G
A7
D
miss you, babe, and I don't wan - na miss a thing.
I don't wan - na
C
G/B
miss one smile. I don't wan - na miss one kiss. I just wan - na
f

I Don't Want to Miss a Thing - 4 - 4

IN DREAMS
(featured in "The Breaking Of The Fellowship")

Words and Music by
FRAN WALSH and
HOWARD SHORE
Arranged by DAN COATES

F C G B♭ Am G F G
walk in bit - ter rain. But in dreams, I can
C G Am G F C
hear your name. And in dreams we will
cresc.
F G Am F C E♭
meet a - gain.
mf
C A♭ E♭ A♭ B♭
mp

C Eb C Ab Bb
rit.
When the
mf
D F#m G D G A
sea and moun - tains fall and we come to end of
a tempo
D A D F#m G D
days, in the dark I hear a call, call - ing me
G D A D
there. I will go there and back a - gain.
rit.
p

Metro-Goldwyn-Mayer Presents David Lean's Film "DOCTOR ZHIVAGO"

SOMEWHERE, MY LOVE

(Lara's Theme from "Doctor Zhivago")

Lyric by
PAUL FRANCIS WEBSTER

Music by
MAURICE JARRE
Arranged by DAN COATES

Am7 D7 Am7 D7 G
al - though the snow cov - ers the hope of spring.
Am7 D7
Some - where a hill blos - soms in green and gold,
Am7 D7 Am7 D7 G
and there are dreams all that your heart can hold.
C G
Some - day we'll meet a - gain my love,
f
B♭ F B♭ D7
some - day when - ev - er the spring breaks through.

G Am7 D7
You'll come to me out of the long a - go,
mf
Am7 D7 Am7 D7 G
warm as the wind, soft as the kiss of snow.
Am7 D7
'Til then, my sweet, think of me now and then,
Am7 D7
God - speed my love
1.
Am7 D7 G
'til you are mine a - gain.
2.
Am7 D7 D7(♭9) G
'til you are mine a - gain.
mp
rit. e dim.
p

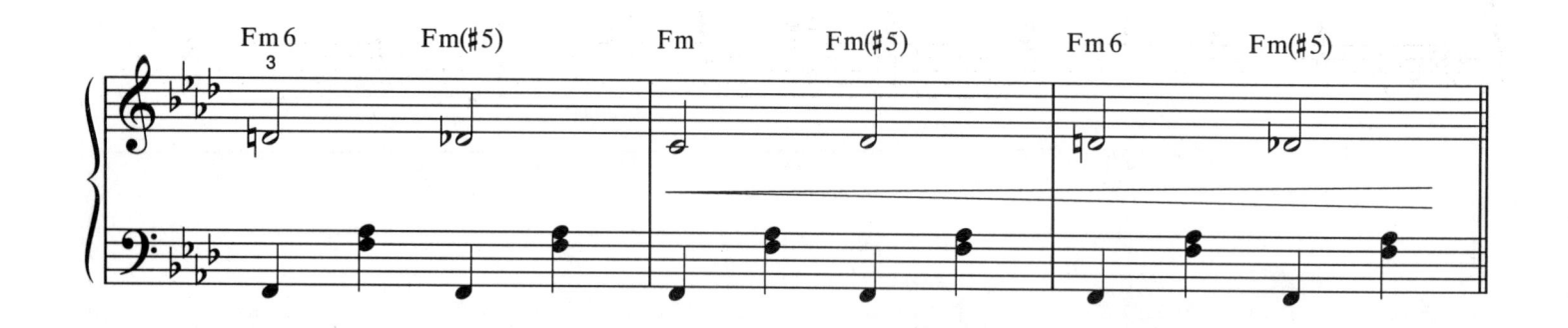

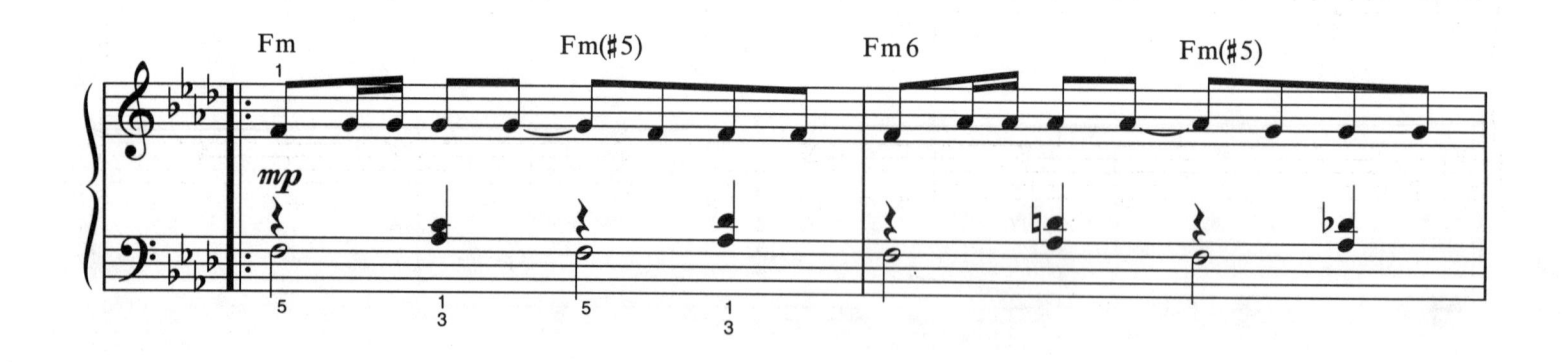

JAMES BOND THEME

Music by
MONTY NORMAN
Arranged by DAN COATES

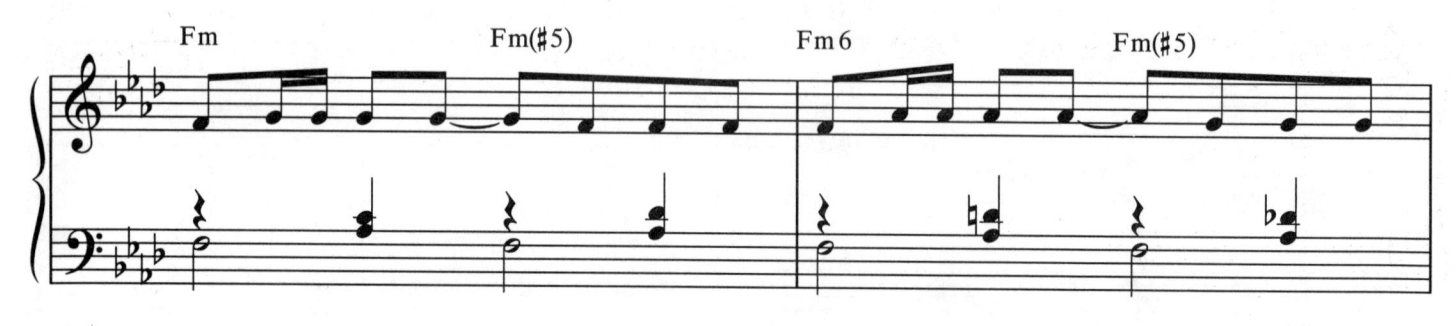

Fm Fm(♯5) Fm6 Fm(♯5)
Fm Fm(♯5) Fm6 Fm(♯5) Fm Fm(♯5)
p
Fm6 Fm(♯5) Fm Fm(♯5) Fm6 Fm(♯5)
With a slight swing feeling
Fm Fm(♯5) Fm6 Fm(♯5) Fm Fm(♯5)
f

Fm6
Fm
Fm(♯5)
Fm6
Fm(♯5)
Fm
Fm(♯5)
Fm6
Fm6
C9
mf
Fm6
C9
Fm6
C9
Fm6
C9
Fm
f
Fm(♯5)
mp
Fm6
Fm(♯5)

Fm
Fm(♯5)
Fm6
Fm(♯5)
mf
Fm
Fm(♯5)
Fm6
Fm(♯5)
Fm
Fm(♯5)
Fm6
Fm(♯5)
Fm
Fm(♯5)
Fm6
Fm(♯5)
N.C.
(R.H.)
cresc.
Fm6(addG)
p

OVER THE RAINBOW

Lyric by
E.Y. HARBURG

Music by
HAROLD ARLEN
Arranged by DAN COATES

Em C7 F C/E C7
o - ver the rain - bow skies are blue,
F Fm C/G A7(♭9) D7 G7
and the dreams that you dare to dream real - ly do come
C6 C F/C G7/C
mp
true. Some day I'll wish up - on a star and wake up where the clouds are far be -
C6 G7 C
mf
hind me, where trou - bles melt like lem - on drops, a -
Edim Em7 E♭dim Dm7 G7(#5)
cresc.
way a - bove the chim - ney tops that's where you'll find me.

C Am Em C7 F C/E C7
Some - where o - ver the rain - bow blue - birds fly,
F Fm C/G A7(♭9) D7 G7
birds fly o - ver the rain - bow, why then, oh why can't
1. C6 G7 2. C6 C
I? I?
G7/C C6 G7
If
C Dm7 G7 C
hap-py lit-tle blue-birds fly be - yond the rain-bow, why oh why can't I?
rit.

SOMEWHERE OUT THERE

Words and Music by
JAMES HORNER, BARRY MANN
and CYNTHIA WEIL
Arranged by DAN COATES

F F/G C C/E F
out there some - one's say - ing a prayer that
Dm7 Em7 Am7 Dm7 C/E F7 F/G
we'll find one an - oth - er in that big some - where_ out
C F G/F F G/F
there. And e - ven though I know how ver - y far a - part we are, it
mf
F G/F F G/F A♭ B♭/A♭
helps to think we might be wish - in' on the same bright star. And when the night wind starts to sing a
A♭ B♭/A♭ A♭ B♭/A♭
lone - some lul - la - by, it helps to think we're sleep - ing un - der -
cresc.

G
C
C/E
neath the same big
sky.
Some - where
f
F
F/G
C
C/E
F
A7
out
there
if
love
can
see us
through,
Dm7
G/F
Em7
Am7
F
then
we'll
be
to -
geth
-
er
some-where
out
there,
out
mf
To Coda
D.S. al Coda
G7
C
where
dreams
come
true.
And
Coda
C
C/E
F
F/G
C
true.
mp
rit. e dim.
p

STAR WARS
(Main Title)

Music by
JOHN WILLIAMS
Arranged by DAN COATES

Star Wars (Main Title) - 2 - 2

STAYIN' ALIVE

Words and Music by
BARRY GIBB,
MAURICE GIBB and ROBIN GIBB
Arranged by DAN COATES

Moderate rock beat, in 2

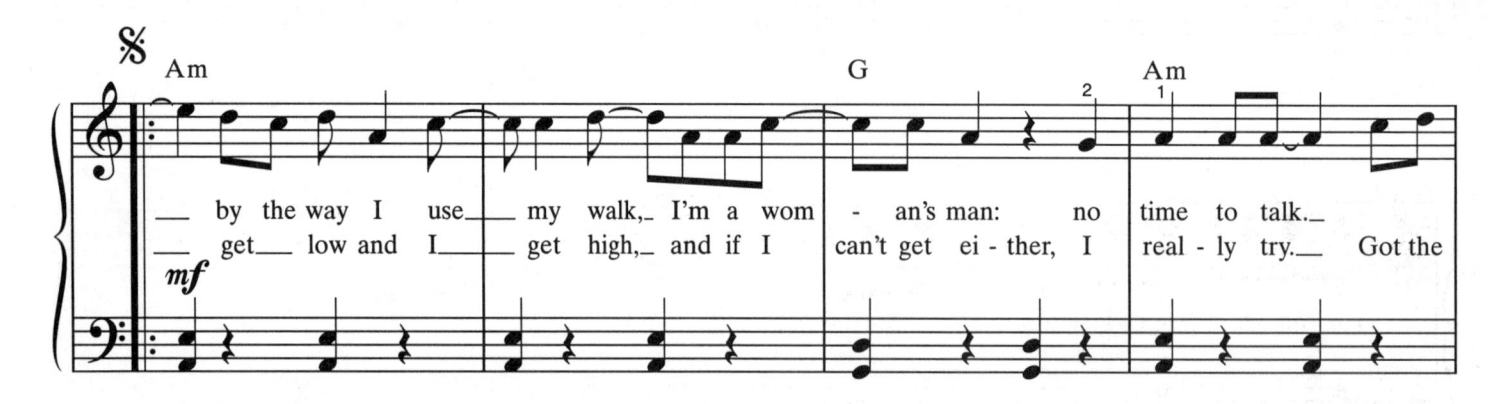

1.3. Well, you can tell ___ by the way I use ___ my walk, I'm a wom - an's man: no time to talk. ___ Got the
    get ___ low and I ___ get high, ___ and if I can't get ei - ther, I real - ly try. ___

Mu - sic loud ___ and wom - en warm, I've been kicked a - round ___ since I ___ was born. ___ And now it's
wings of heav - en on ___ my shoes. I'm a danc - in' man ___ and I just can't lose. ___ You know it's

all right. ___ It's O. K. ___ And you may look ___ the oth - er way. ___
all right. ___ It's O. K. ___ I'll live to see ___ an - oth - er day. ___

© 1977 CROMPTON SONGS LLC and GIBB BROTHERS MUSIC
All Rights for CROMPTON SONGS LLC Administered by WARNER-TAMERLANE PUBLISHING CORP.
All Rights Reserved

Stayin' Alive - 4 - 1

We can try to under - stand the New York Times' ef - fect on man.
cresc.
Am7
Wheth-er you're a broth-er or wheth - er you're a moth-er, you're stay - in' a - live,
stay - in' a - live.
f
Feel the cit - y break-in' and ev - 'ry-bod - y shak-in' and we're stay - in' a - live,
stay - in' a - live.
Ah, ha, ha, ha, stay-in' a - live,
stay-in' a - live.
Ah, ha, ha, ha, stay - in' a - live.

G/A
dim.
Am
mf
Em7
To Coda
Am7
f
1.
2.
2. Well, now I
D7
mf
Life go - in' no - where.
Some - bod - y help me.
Some - bod - y help me, yeah.
Am7

D7
Life go - in' no - where.
Some - bod - y help_ me, yeah.
Am7
f
D.S. 𝄋 al Coda
3. Well, you can tell
Coda
Am7
f
Em7
Am
I'm stay-in' a - live.
ff

TEARS IN HEAVEN

Words and Music by
ERIC CLAPTON and WILL JENNINGS
Arranged by DAN COATES

B/D♯ G7/D E D/F♯ E/G♯
strong and car - ry on, 'cause I
way through night and day, 'cause I
Am D7sus4 D G D/F♯
know I don't be - long here in heav - en.
know I just can't stay here in heav - en.
Em G/D C/E D7 1.G
p
2. G
p
B♭ Am Gm C/E
mf
Time can bring you down, time can bend your knees.

F C/E Dm C/E F B♭ Am
Time can break your heart,
Gm C/E F D C/E D/F♯
have you beg - ging, "Please!" Beg - ging, "Please!"
G D/F♯ Em G/D C/E G/D
mp
(Piano solo...
Would you know my name if I saw you in heav -
D G/D D7 G D/F♯ Em G/D
en? Would you be the same

Tears in Heaven - 4 - 4

THAT'S WHAT FRIENDS ARE FOR

Words and Music by
BURT BACHARACH and CAROLE BAYER SAGER
Arranged by DAN COATES

B7sus4 B7 Em7 Cmaj7
got the chance to say that I do be - lieve I
so much more I see. And so by the way I
Am7/D G Bm7 Em7
love you. And if I should ev - er go a -
thank you. And then for the times when we're a -
mf
Am7
way, well then close your eyes and
part, well then close your eyes and
F#m7 B7sus4 B7 Em7
try to feel the way we do to - day.
know these words are com - ing from my heart.
And then

Cmaj7
Am7/D
D7
if you can — re - mem - ber, —
cresc.
G
G/F♯
f
keep smil - ing,
keep shin - ing,
C
D7/C
Bm7
know - ing you — can
al - ways count on
me — for
Em7
Cmaj7
Am7/D
D9
sure,
that's what friends — are
for.

G
G/F♯
For good times
In good times,
and bad times
in bad times
F6
E7sus4
E7
I'll be on your
side for - ev - er
E♭6
D7sus4
To Coda
more.
That's what friends are
D. S. al Coda
1.
2.
D7
D7
Cmaj7/D
D7
for.
for.

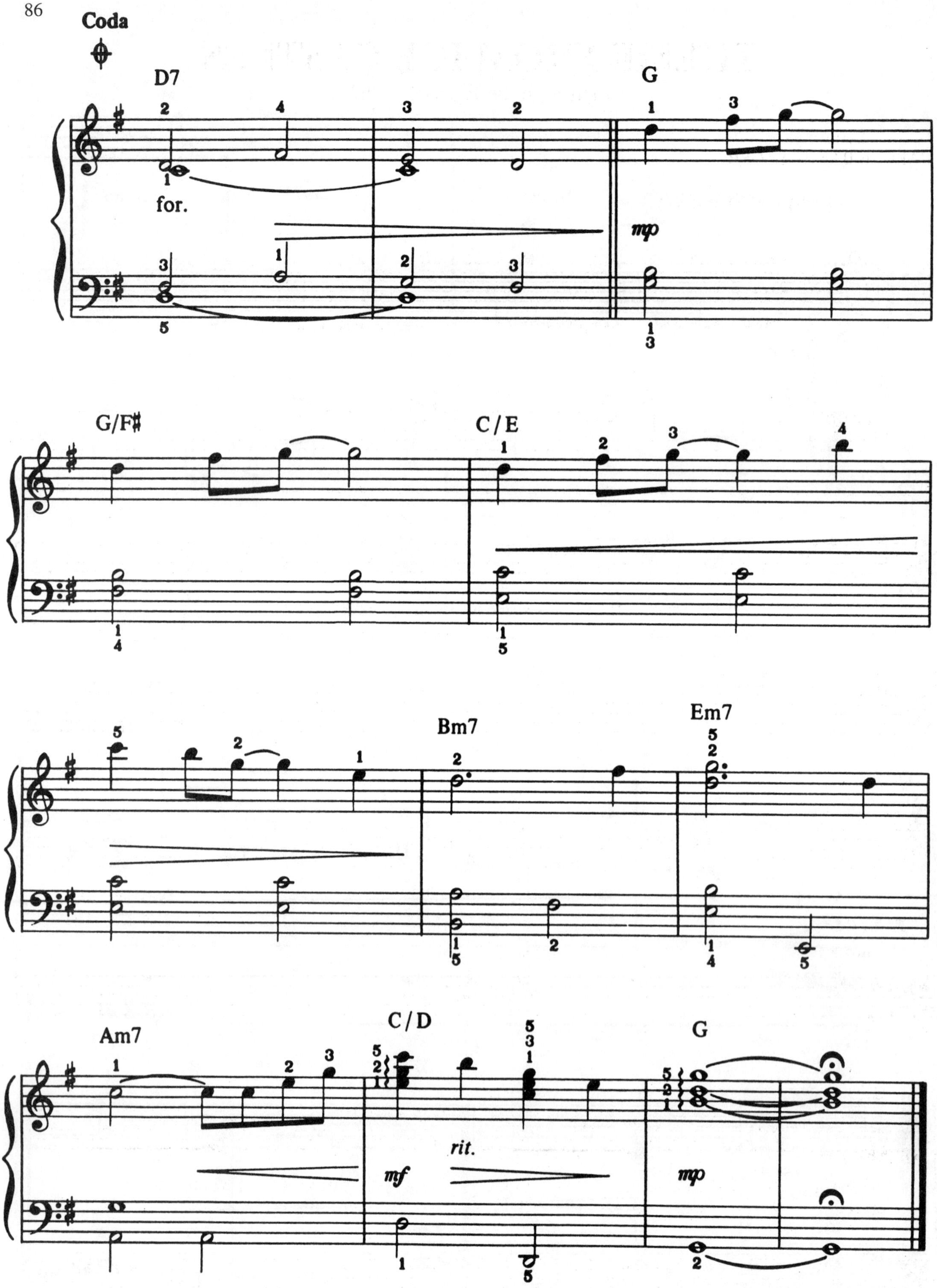
Coda
D7
G
for.
mp
G/F♯
C/E
Bm7
Em7
Am7
C/D
G
mf
rit.
mp

THEME FROM ICE CASTLES
(Through the Eyes of Love)

Lyrics by
CAROLE BAYER SAGER

Music by
MARVIN HAMLISCH
Arranged by DAN COATES

Slowly, with feeling

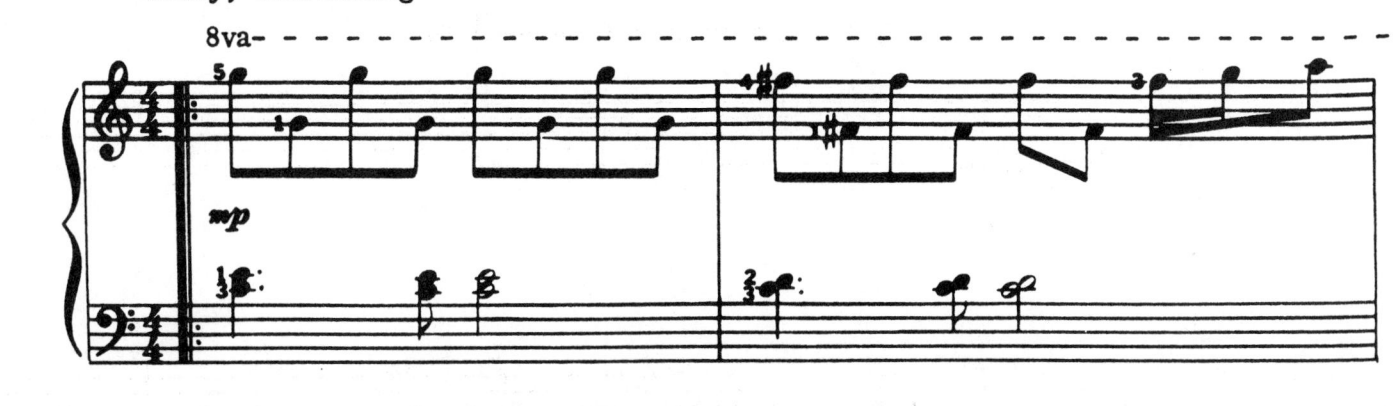

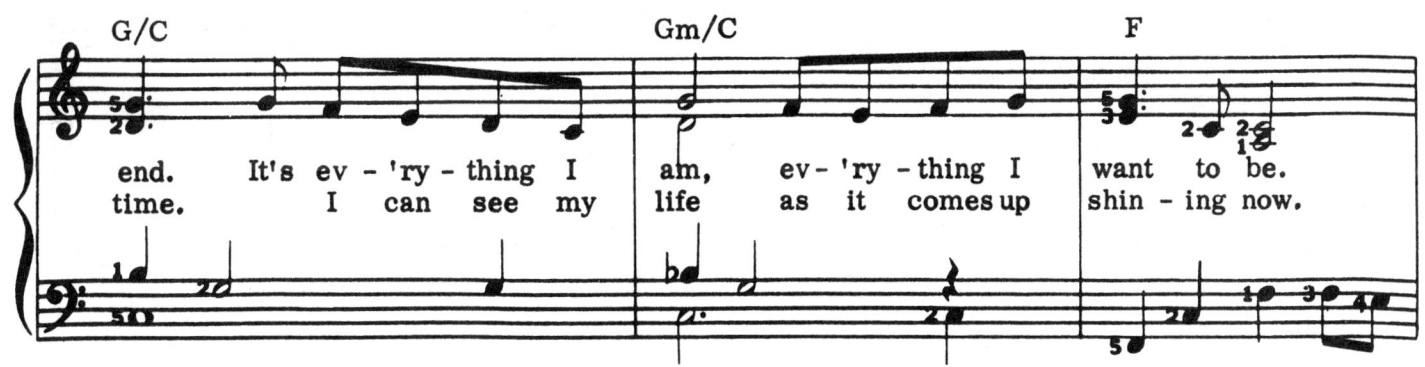

Lyrics:
1. Please, don't let this feel-ing end. It's ev-'ry-thing I am, ev-'ry-thing I want to be.
   now, I can take the time. I can see my life as it comes up shin-ing now.

Theme From Ice Castles - 3 - 1

© 1978 EMI GOLD HORIZON MUSIC CORP. and EMI GOLDEN TORCH MUSIC CORP.
All Rights Reserved

Dm G G7/F Em7 Am7 Dm G G7/F
I can see what's mine now, find - ing out what's
Reach-ing out to touch you, I can feel so
To Coda
Em7 Am7 F E7 Am D9
true / much since I found you look - ing
1.
Dm7 G7
through the eyes of love. 2. And
2.
Dm G7 C Am
through the eyes of love. And now I

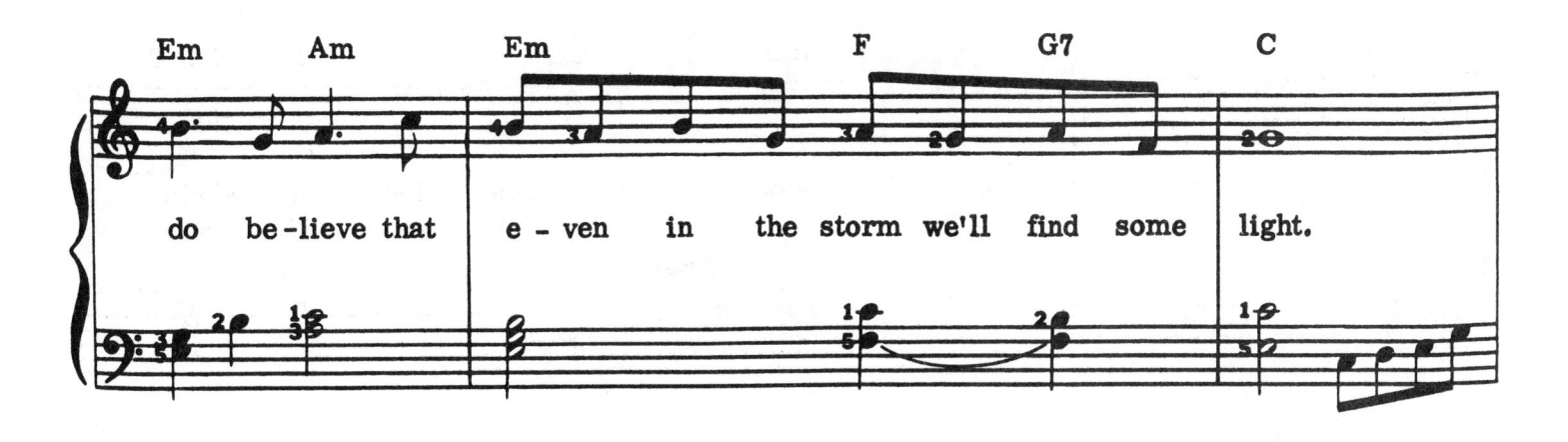

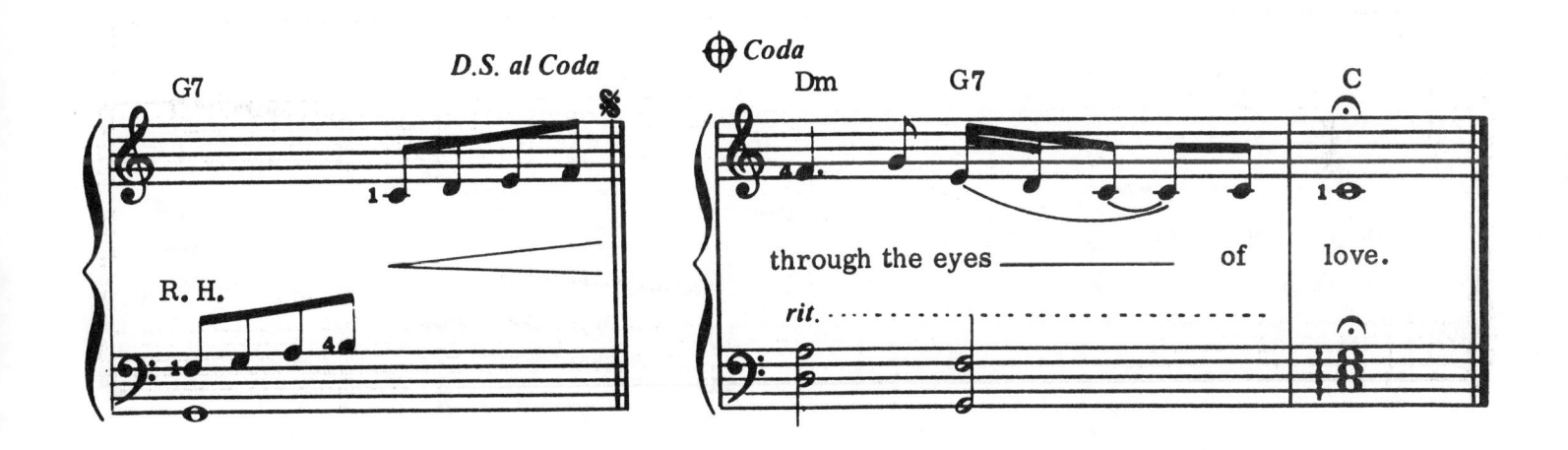

3. Please, don't let this feeling end.
   It might not come again
   And I want to remember
   How it feels to touch you
   How I feel so much
   Since I found you
   Looking through the eyes of love.

From Touchstone Pictures' "PEARL HARBOR"

THERE YOU'LL BE

Words and Music by
DIANE WARREN
Arranged by DAN COATES

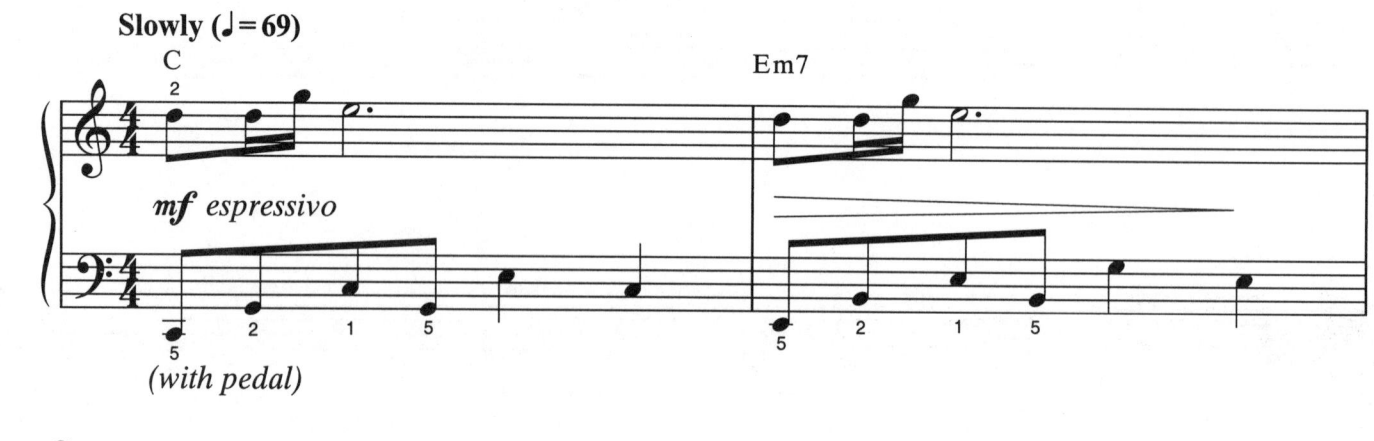

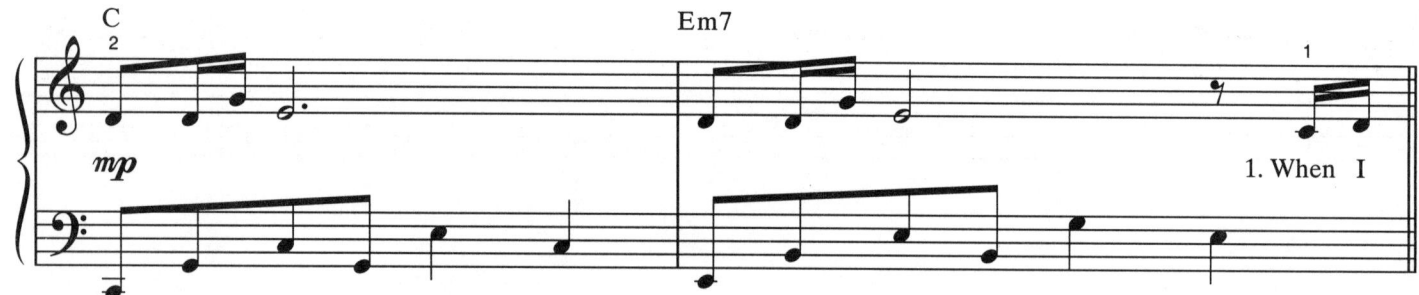

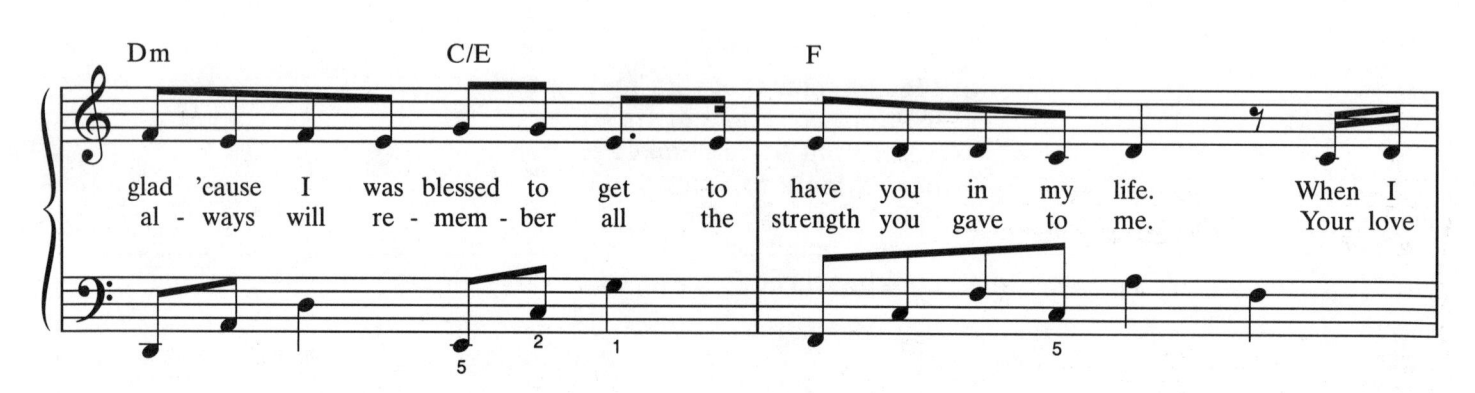

Slowly (♩ = 69)

mf espressivo

(with pedal)

mp

Verse:

think back on these times and the dreams we left be-hind, I'll be
showed me how it feels to feel the sky with-in my reach. And I

glad 'cause I was blessed to get to have you in my life. When I
al-ways will re-mem-ber all the strength you gave to me. Your love

There You'll Be - 5 - 1

© 2001 REALSONGS (ASCAP)
All Rights Reserved

C G/B F
look back on these days, I'll look and see your face.
made me make it through. I owe so much to you.
C/E Bb/D C/E F G
You were right there for me.
Chorus:
Am Em/G F C/E
In my dreams I'll al - ways see you soar a - bove the sky.
Am Em/G F G
In my heart there'll al - ways be a place for you for all my life.

C G/B Am G
I'll keep a part of you with me. And
1.
F C/E Dm7 C
ev - 'ry - where I am, there you'll be. And
F C/E Dm7 C B♭ F/A
ev - 'ry - where I am, there you'll be. 2. Well, you
2.
F C/E Dm7 G C
ev - 'ry - where I am, there you'll be. 'Cause I al - ways saw in you my

F/A G/B C G C
light, my strength.
And I want to thank you now for
Am7 F C/E
all the ways
you were right there for me.
B♭/D C/E F G
You were right there for me for
cresc.
al - ways.
Am Em/G F C/E
f
In my dreams I'll al - ways see you
soar a - bove the sky.

Dm7 G F G
In my heart there'll al - ways be a place for you for all my life.
C G/B Am G
ff
I'll keep a part of you with me. And
F C/E Dm7 C F C/E Dm7 C
ev - 'ry - where I am, there you'll be. And ev - 'ry - where I am, there you'll be.
mf
B♭ C(9)
There you'll be.
rit. e dim.
mp

THE WIND BENEATH MY WINGS

Words and Music by
LARRY HENLEY and JEFF SILBAR
Arranged by DAN COATES

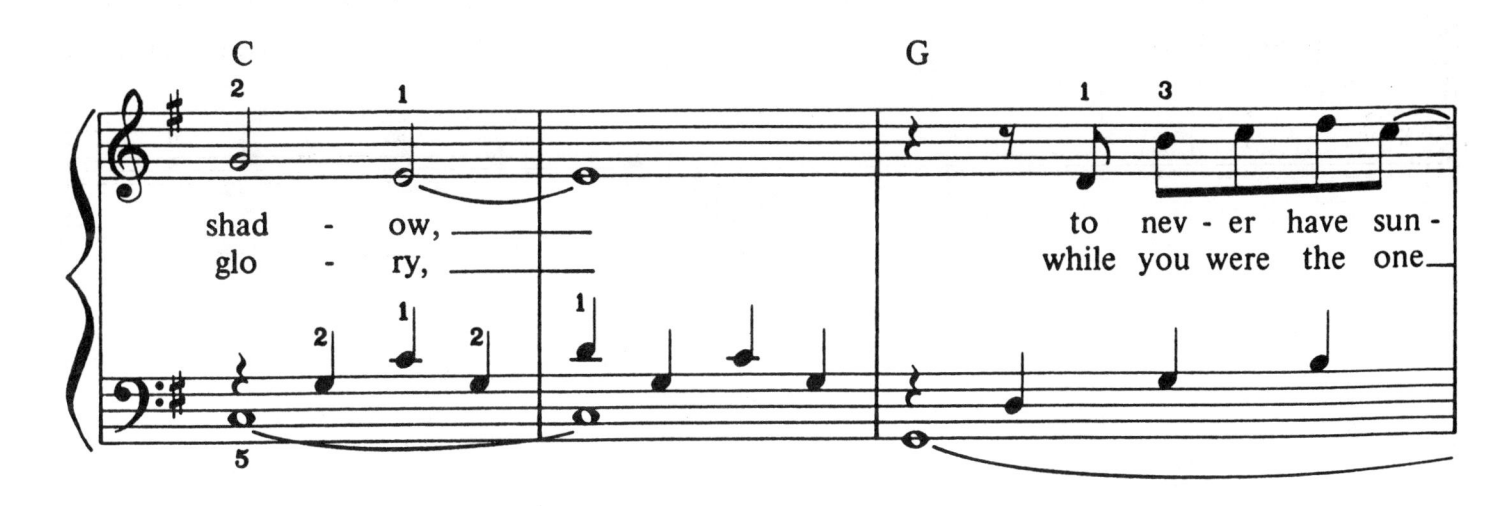

1. It must have been cold there, my shad-ow, to nev-er have sun-
2. I was the one with all the glo-ry, while you were the one

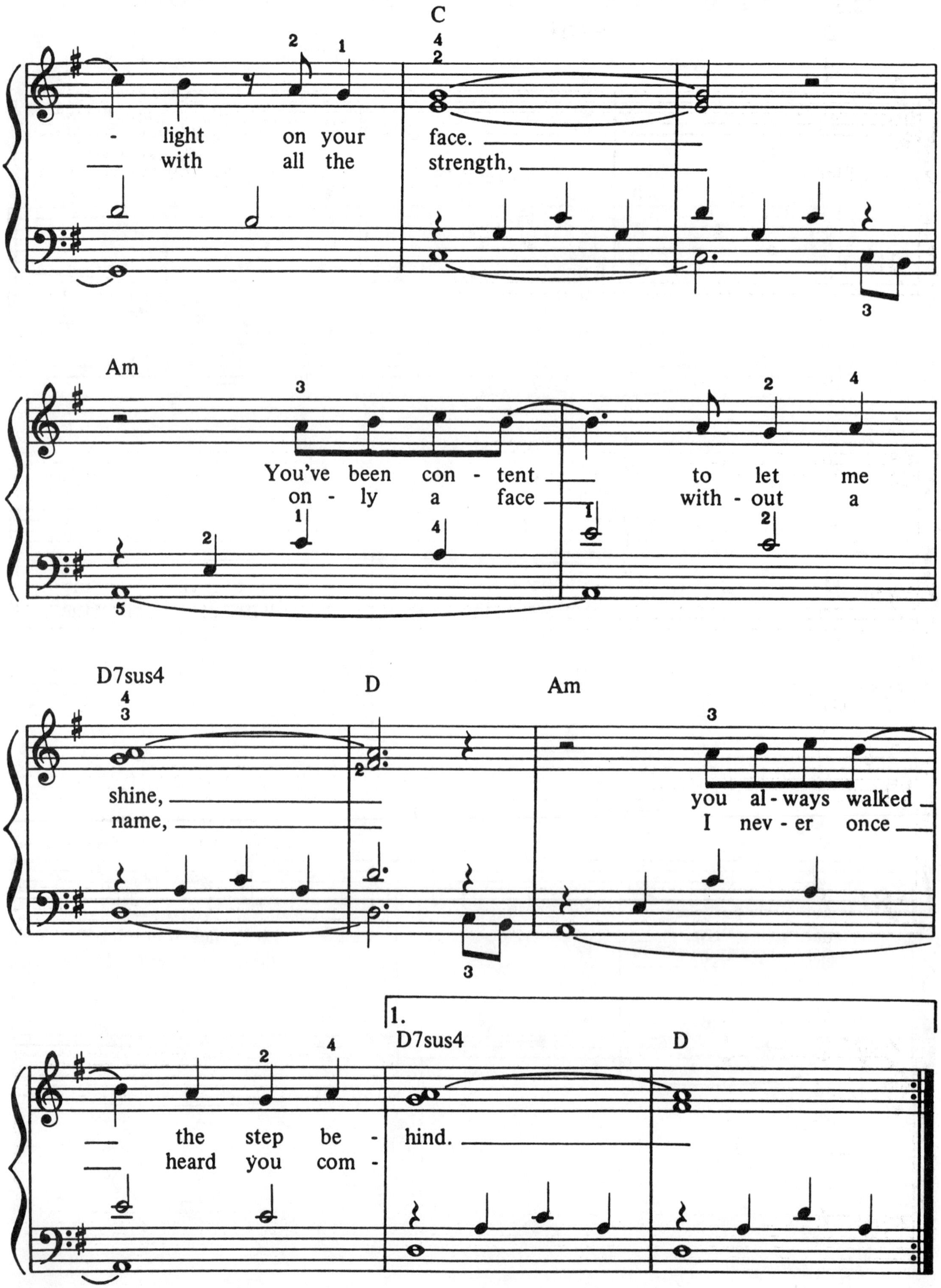
C
- light on your face.
with all the strength,
Am
You've been con - tent to let me
on - ly a face with - out a
D7sus4
D
Am
shine,
name,
you al - ways walked
I nev - er once
1.
D7sus4
D
the step be - hind.
heard you com -

97

D/F♯
C/E
D
Em
f
I can fly high-
C
- er than an
Em7
ea -
E7(♭9)
gle,
Am
mp
'cause you are the wind ___ be-neath my
Am7/D
D7
To Coda
G
wings.
D. S. 𝄋 al Coda
C

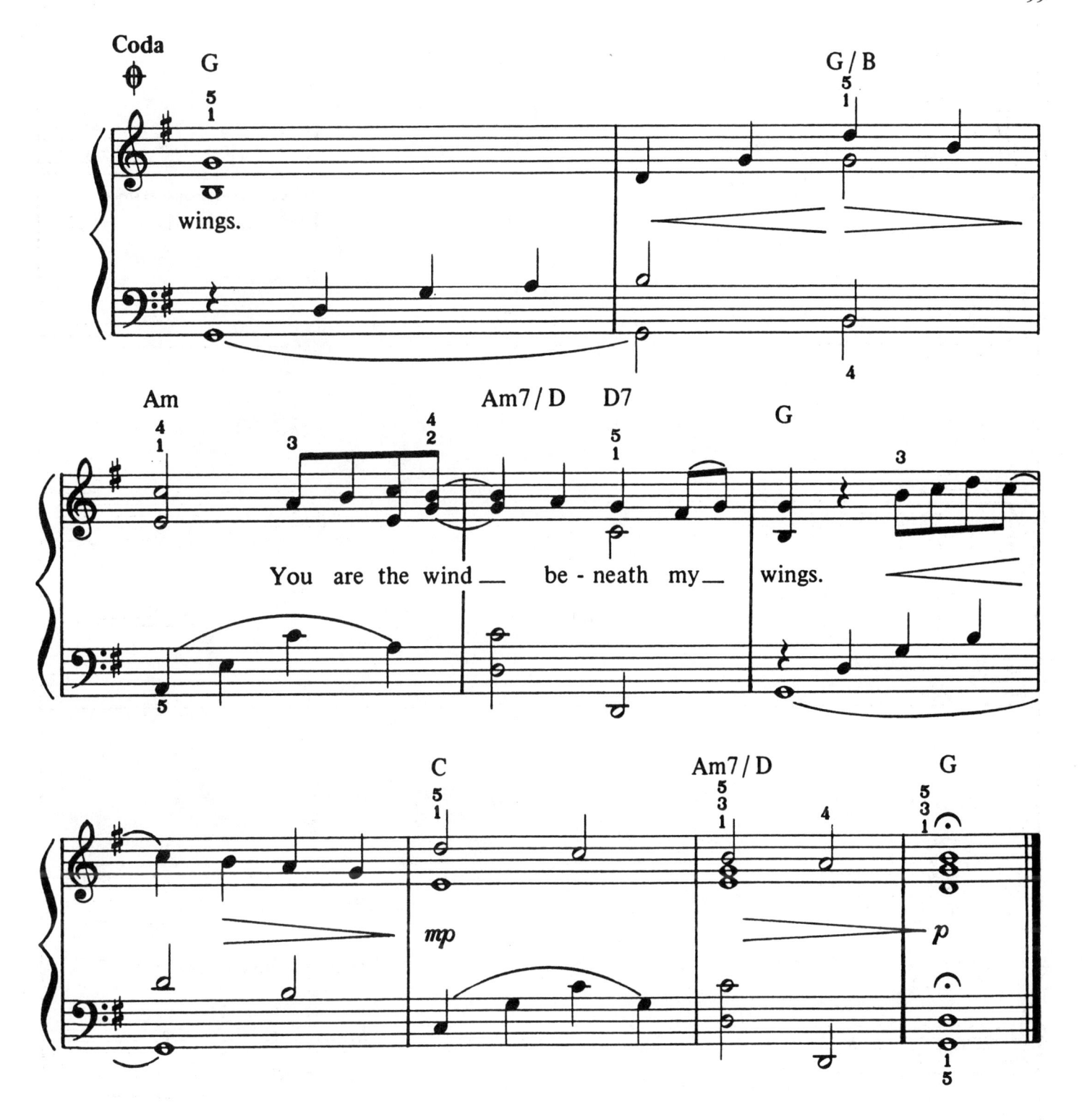

3. It might have appeared to go unnoticed
that I've got it all here in my heart.
I want you to know I know the truth:
I would be nothing without you.

Dan Coates...
The Best in Easy Piano

A Decade of Lite Hits: Contemporary Pop Ballads
(AFM00031)
A wonderful collection of some of the most beautiful pop ballads of the last decade expertly arranged by Dan Coates. Titles include: All My Life • Amazed • Angel Eyes • Back at One • Because of You • Candle in the Wind • Don't Cry for Me Argentina • From This Moment On • I Believe I Can Fly • I Do (Cherish You) • I Turn to You • In This Life • Love Will Keep Us Alive • The One • Sand & Water • Smooth • Sunny Came Home and many more.

The Hits of Elton John
(AFM01010)
Lush Dan Coates arrangements of 14 of Elton John's signature tunes including: Candle in the Wind • Daniel • Don't Let the Sun Go Down on Me • Little Jeannie • Nikita • The One • Sacrifice • Sad Songs (Say So Much) • Something About the Way You Look Tonight • Sorry Seems to Be the Hardest Word • Tiny Dancer • Your Song and more.

Pop Music Hits 2001
(AFM01016)
Twenty-five of the hottest pop hits by such artists as Lonestar, Faith Hill, Christina Aguilera, 98°, Jessica Simpson, Britney Spears, Backstreet Boys, Brian McKnight, ★NSYNC and more. Titles include: Amazed • Breathe • Come On Over (All I Want Is You) • Give Me Just One Night • I Think I'm in Love with You • I Turn to You • Lucky • My Everything • Shape of My Heart • Show Me the Meaning of Being Lonely • Stronger • That's the Way It Is • This I Promise You • Win and more.

Something More for the Boys
(AFM01007)
Music and songs from cartoons, movies, and television, as well as classic rock, modern rock, pop, and much more — titles that boys will really like! Titles include: American Pie • Change the World • Just Give Me One Night (Una Noche) • Hotel California • Lean on Me • (Meet) The Flintstones • "Jetsons" Main Theme • Olympic Fanfare and Theme • Smooth • Theme from *Inspector Gadget* and more!

Something More for the Girls
(AFM01008)
A fantastic collection of 21 songs that are favorites of today's pre-teen and teenage girls. They'll love the titles, which are straight from the top of the charts. Titles include: Graduation (Friends Forever) • I Hope You Dance • I Think I'm in Love with You • Lucky • Oops!...I Did It Again • Shape of My Heart • Stronger • That's the Way It Is • This I Promise You • A Whole New World and more!